New English Grammar for ESL Students

By

Fritz-Meyer Sannon, PhD.

© 2004 by Fritz-Meyer Sannon, PhD. All rights reserved.

No part of this book may be reproduced, stored in a retrieval system, or transmitted by any means, electronic, mechanical, photocopying, recording, or otherwise, without written permission from the author.

ISBN: 1-4107-9184-X (e-book)
ISBN: 1-4107-9183-1 (Paperback)
ISBN: 1-4107-9182-3 (Dust Jacket)

Library of Congress Control Number: 2003096498

This book is printed on acid free paper.

Printed in the United States of America
Bloomington, IN

1stBooks - rev. 02/16/04

New English Grammar

and Exercises
for
ESL Students

(Beginner-intermediate-advanced)

Including

100 Ephemisms. 200 Troublesome words in American English.

100 Proverbs, 200 Idiomatic expressions
(in English, in Spanish, in French.)

This manual is an indispensable tool for
high school and college students, professionals and
office workers.

by

Fritz-Meyer Sannon, PhD.

To the students of **The State University of New York/Queens EOC** who have shown respect, admiration and love for all their instructors…

To those around the world who finally recognize that **the English language** is an important tool for international communication,

I dedicate this **"New English Grammar."**

Fritz-Meyer Sannon, PhD

I thank my son Lionel Sannon and his wife Jocelyne; my son Philip Sannon and his wife Jessica; my son Frantz Sannon and my grand-son Leonard Sannon for their support.

To my daughter, Fritzy Sannon-Brown, Assistant Principal of the Island Academy High School and Lecturer at Laguardia Community College, I am grateful for her assistance and enthusiasm.

I thank especially, my fifteen-year old son Richard Sannon for his excellent work in typing the first draft of this manual.

Without their financial support this manual would not be published.

To Carline Keil who had helped me with the proof reading, I am thankful for her commitment and her dedication.

To Snide Franck for his cooperation. Snide is working towards his Master Degree in French at Brooklyn College.

Table of Contents

Preface xxi

Chapter 1 Parts of Speech 3
Articles 5
DEFINITE ARTICLES AND EXERCISES
The (two pronunciations)
INDEFINITE ARTICLES AND EXERCISES
Exercises 15

Chapter 2 Nouns (DEFINITION) 23
Different Kinds of Nouns:
Common Nouns – Proper Nouns – Concrete Nouns
Abstract Nouns – Mass Nouns – Count Nouns
Compound Nouns – Collective Nouns
Irregular Plural of Nouns
Possessive Case
Homonyms – Homographs – Homophones
Synonyms
Antonyms
Exercises 38

Chapter 3 Adjectives (DEFINITION) 47
Different Kinds of Adjectives:
Descriptive Adjectives
Possessive Adjectives
Demonstrative Adjectives
Numeral Cardinal Adjectives
Numeral Ordinal Adjectives

    Interrogative Adjectives
    Indefinite Adjectives
    Adjectives (or noun as modifiers)
    Degrees of the Adjectives
    Comparative Degree
    Superlative Degree
    Exercises..64

Chapter 4 Pronouns (DEFINITION) 71
    Different Kinds of Pronouns:
    Personal Pronouns (subject + object)
    Pronouns Versus Adjectives
    Possessive Adjectives vs. Possessive Pronouns
    Demonstrative Adjectives vs. Demonstrative Pronouns
    Interrogative Adjectives vs. Interrogative Pronouns
    Indefinite Adjectives vs. Indefinite Pronouns
    Relative Pronouns
    Reflexive Pronouns
    Reciprocal Pronouns
    Exercises..86

Chapter 5 Verbs (DEFINITION)...................109
    Classification of Verbs
    Auxiliary Verbs (to be, to have)
    Expressions with Verbs To Be
    Expressions with Verbs to Have
    Classes and Types of Verbs
    Regular Verbs
    Irregular Verbs
    Transitive Verbs
    Intransitive Verbs

Action Verbs and Non-Action Verbs
    Exercises *117*
    Exercises *145*
    Exercises *155*

Chapter 6 Periphrastic Modals and Linking Verbs ... 165
    Exercises *173*

Chapter 7 Mood/Tenses of Verbs 181
  Infinitive
  Participle
  Indicative
  Imperative
  Subjunctive
  Progressive Forms (or present continuous)
  Present Perfect
  Past Perfect
  Future Perfect
  Conditional
  Passive Voice
  Present-Past-Future-Conditional
  Sequence of Tenses
  Present – Different Uses
  Exercises *206*

Chapter 8 Adverbs 217
  Adverbs of Degree
  Adverbs of Duration
  Adverbs of Emphasis
  Adverbs of Frequency
  Adverbs of Interrogation
  Adverbs of Manner

Mid-Sentence Adverbs
Adverbs of Place
Adverbs of Probabilities
Adverbs of Time
Conjunctive Adverbs
Exercises..231

Chapter 9 What is a sentence? 241
Simple Sentences
Compound Sentences
Complex Sentences
Compound/Complex Sentences
Declarative Sentences
Imperative Sentences
Interrogative Sentences
Negative Sentences
Exclamatory Sentences
Conditional Sentences
Exercises..259

Chapter 10 Parts of a sentence (continued) 269
The clause..269
Independent Clause
Main Clause
Subordinate Clause
1 – Subordinate Clauses as Adjective Clauses
2 – Subordinate Clauses as Noun Clauses
3 – Subordinate Clauses as Adverbial Clauses
Exercises..285

Chapter 11 Parts of a Sentence (continued)................297
The Phrase..297

Appositive Phrases
Gerund Phrases
Infinitive Phrases
Noun Phrases
Participial Phrases
Prepositional Phrases
Verbal Phrases
Exercises *313*

Chapter 12 Object Completing Element 325
Direct Object
Indirect Object
Object of a Preposition
Object of a Verbal (gerund, participle, infinitive)
Pronouns as Objects
Object of Verbal (gerund, infinitive, etc.)
Exercises *334*

Chapter 13 Prepositions 341
Different Kinds of Prepositions
Exercises *353*

Chapter 14 Conjunctions 361
Coordinating Conjunction
Correlative Conjunction
Conjunctive Adverbs
Subordinating Conjunction
Exercises *371*

Chapter 15 Interjections 381
Exercises *386*

Chapter 16 Punctuation 393

Appendix A Euphemisms 413
    EUPHEMISMS (DEFINITION)
    Listing of Most Common Euphemisms

Appendix B 423
    Listing of 200 Troublesome Words in English

Appendix C 445
    Listing of 100 American Proverbs and their
    Equivalent in Spanish and French

Appendix D 459
    Listing of 200 American Idioms and their Equivalent
    in Spanish and French

Appendix E 477
    U. S. States and Capitals

Table of Illustrations

THE CAPITOL WASHINGTON, D.C., U.S.A. 1

CHURCH OF SAN FRANCISCO, QUITO, ECUADOR 21

INDIAN PROCESSION FIESTA OF NUESTRA SENORA DE LOS ANGELES, GUATEMALA 45

ESL STUDENT'S BACKYARD IN CHALOITENANGO, EL SALVADOR 69

UNIVERSITY OF LOS ANDES MERIDA, VENEZUELA 107

LEGENDARY CITADEL ONE OF THE WONDERS OF THE WORLD, HAITI 163

TYPES OF HOUSES IN THE OLD PORT-AU-PRINCE, HAITI 179

MUSEUM OF ART PONCE, PUERTO RICO 215

PRIMITIVE FARMING METHOD USED BY ANDEAN FARMERS PERU 239

WINTER IN QUEBEC CITY, CANADA MON DIEU! C'EST TERRIBLE! 267

16TH CENTURY RUIN IN OLD PANAMA, PANAMA 295

OFFICE BUILDING IN PLACE DE L'INDEPENDENCE DAKAR, SENEGAL (AFRICA) 323

PLACE DE LA REPUBLIQUE ABIDJAN, IVORY COAST (AFRICA) 339

KABUL, AFGHANISTAN (BEFORE THE WAR 2001) 359

THE HOUSE OF CHRISTOPHER COLUMBUS (DOMINICAN REPUBLIC) 379

NATIONAL THEATER IN SAN SALVADOR EL SALVADOR 391

DO YOU LIKE SQUIRRELS? REALLY? 411

THESE ARE RACCOONS. THEY ARE BEAUTIFUL. 421

CATS LIKE PEOPLE 443

ME AGAIN, MR. SQUIRREL 457

WHO IS YOUR BETTER FRIEND, MICKEY OR JANET? 475

Preface

After thirty-two years of translating and teaching Latin, French, Spanish and English, I am convinced that most of the modern western languages share <u>about</u> the same syntactic structures. For a long, long time, I had been thinking about writing a Manual of Etiquette for the benefit of the ESL learners throughout the United States of America, especially for the students of the State University of New York/Queens EOC (York College) where I have been teaching for more than 12 years. Sincerely, I have no ambition to cover all components of the grammar such as <u>Morphology</u> which deals with the variations of the forms of words; <u>Phonology</u> that refers to the rules and principles behind sound shifts during the history and development of the languages; or <u>Semantics</u>, the study of meanings explaining how sentences are understood.

My objective is to focus on <u>Syntax</u>, the study of relations of words to one another. This project is more or less a review of the parts of speech and the parts of a sentence, meaning a listing, a definition and an explanation of each part of speech from articles (definite and indefinite), adjectives through interjections and signs of punctuation, without leaving out the verbs, adverbs, prepositions and conjunctions (coordinating, correlative and subordinating). In addition, I will emphasize on the parts of a sentence by explaining in detail the role and function of the phrases (noun phrases, gerund phrases, adjective phrases, etc.) The role and functions of the clause (independent, dependent) and of the use, the limits and the kinds of sentences (affirmative, exclamative, imperative, etc.) used in mainstream English, with full examples followed by appropriate exercises.

I am aware that this textbook follows the trend of traditional Greco-Roman perspective which has been challenged by modern linguistic theories around the world. However, I am confident that the New English Grammar for ESL Students will be an invaluable asset to people who want to learn a foreign language.

My intention is to target the huge Spanish population without the exclusion of the other ethnicities, and the manual is designed not only for the foreigners who have had difficulties in expressing themselves in the main stream language, but also for the common Americans who do not have the linguistic competence of the standard dialect. Because our schools, at all levels, fail to teach "English grammar", this manual will be a useful tool for high school, college students, for professionals and even for the office workers who are unable to write a formal memo to their immediate supervisors.

Since my target population is mostly Spanish and French speaking people, I include a listing of 200 <u>American idioms</u> and 100 <u>American proverbs</u> with their translation in Spanish and French.

This manual will be a good teaching material for instructors and learners.

Fritz-Meyer Sannon, Ph.D.

New English Grammar for ESL Students

The Capitol
Washington, D. C.
USA

Fritz-Meyer Sannon, PhD.

Chapter 1

Parts of Speech

Definition: Parts of speech are the ways words are divided according to their relation (or function) to sentence structures.

There are about eight parts of speech:

Nouns, adjectives, pronouns, verbs, adverbs, prepositions, conjunctions, interjections. In all languages (modern or ancient) there are what we call parts of speech. Some languages have less than others.

In the **"New English Grammar for ESL Students"** we distinguish 10 parts of speech which are:

  1 - **Articles** * (the, a, an)

  2 - **Nouns** (boy, girl, table, Peru, etc.)

Fritz-Meyer Sannon, PhD.

    3 - **Adjectives** (clean, beautiful, ugly, smart, etc.)

    4 - **Pronouns** (you, she, we, they, etc.)

    5 - **Verbs** (to leave, to go, to study, to win, etc.)

    6 - **Adverbs** (frequently, fast, very, too, etc.)

    7 - **Prepositions** (at, under, on, after, etc.)

    8 - **Conjunctions** (and, or, but, because, etc.)

    9 - **Interjections** (oh! wow! alas! gosh! etc.)

    10- **Punctuation** (?, :,;, [], etc.)

*Note: Some languages such as Japanese, Russian, Latin, etc. have no articles.

Articles

Definition: What is an article? An article (from Latin, articulus) is a word placed before a noun to limit or define its application. Articles are members of a group of words called determiners. There are in English two kinds of articles: the definite article and the indefinite article.

DEFINITE ARTICLES AND EXERCISES

The (two pronunciations)

The definite article is "THE" for the singular and plural.

(Singular) The horse; the boy; the man.

(Plural) The horses; the boys; the men.

- **The indefinite article** is *"a"* or *"an."* We use *"a"* before a noun beginning with a consonant sound.

Fritz-Meyer Sannon, PhD.

Example: A boy; a school; a desk.

We use "*an*" before a noun beginning with a vowel sound.

Example: An eye; an uncle; an egg.

Please note that the definite article *"the"* is used before singular or plural count nouns which are identified. We mean by count nouns – as we have already seen – nouns that we can count (one, two, three, etc.).

Examples: The teachers (correct)

    The blackboards (correct)

    The students (correct)

    The ice-cream (incorrect)

    The water (incorrect)

    The rice (incorrect)

The definite article is pronounced [ði] before a vowel sound and [ðe] before a consonant sound.

[ði] apple, the end, the only boy, the uncle, the eye, the orange, etc.

[ðe] brother, the professor, the book, the school, the lesson, the boy, etc.

Remark: Even though the noun starts with a vowel, it does not mean that the noun starts with a vowel sound.

Examples:

    a) *The United States of America.*

    b) *The University of the State of New York*

    c) *The one who came first.*

In the three examples above (a, b, c) *"the"* is pronounced [ðe].

We can also use the definite article "the" (pronounced) ði to indicate that a person or thing is exceptional.

Examples:

    a) *This gentlemen is "the" doctor.* [ði]

Fritz-Meyer Sannon, PhD.

 b) *"The" professor.* [ði]

 c) *"The" dentist.* [ði]

 d) *"The" carpenter.* [ði]

In the examples (a, b, c, d) *"the"* is pronounced [ ] (thee).

INDEFINITE ARTICLES AND EXERCISES

Indefinite article is *"a"* or *"an"* for the singular only, not for the plural form. The indefinite article denotes one of a class or number without specifying which one.

Examples: A garden, a donkey, a mountain, or an apple, an eye, an egg.

Please note the indefinite article is not used before a plural noun. Like the definite article, the indefinite article is commonly used before a count noun, not before a mass noun. (Of course there are a few exceptions.)

Some examples with indefinite articles:

A teacher (correct)

A blackboard (correct)

A student (correct)

An uncle (correct)

An eye, etc. (correct)

But: *A water (incorrect)*

A rice (incorrect)

An oil (incorrect)

It is very important to remember that the definite article (the) can be omitted even before count nouns, especially:

a) Nouns used in general sense

b) Names of countries, states, streets, etc.

c) Names of languages

d) Names of titles

e) After both and "all" and before "last" and "next"

f) Before nouns used as adjectives

g) In various expressions

A) Nouns used in general sense:

1 – Courage is a virtue. (No article) but we say: He has the courage to do it.

2 – Coffee has too much caffeine. (No article) but we say: The coffee of Puerto Rico, "el bustelo", is very good.

3 – Patience is very important to be a good teacher. (No article) Mr. Fritz has the patience of a good teacher.

B) Names of countries (or cities, lakes, streets)

1. – Africa is a big and beautiful continent.
2. – My friend Franz is going to Havana, Cuba sometime next week.
3. – Brazil is one of the largest countries in South America.
4. – She lives on Jamaica Avenue.

However: We say the United Arab Emirates, the USA, the USSR, The People's Republic of China.

C) Names of Languages:

French is a very beautiful language. Spanish and Italian are also two romantic languages.

But we say: We think that the French language is not difficult and it is enjoyable to study the Italian or the Spanish language.

D) Titles preceding names of people:

1. – President Kennedy said, "Ask not what your country can do for you, ask what you can do for your country."

2. – General Leclerc and his troops invaded Saint Dominique.

3. – Captain Jorge went to Baranquilla.

But, we can say: The President of the United States went to Europe or The general of the Army is really crazy…or The captain, the commanding officer, just gave order to bombard the ship over there.

Fritz-Meyer Sannon, PhD.

E) After the words "all" and "both" and before "last" and "next"

Examples:

>*All (the) seven students left the room.*
>
>*Both (the) instructors are absent tonight.*
>
>*Last Sunday I was in Hinche.*
>
>*Last year Xiomara went to Tegucigalpa.*
>
>*Next year, Carmen will be in Santiago.*
>
>*But people say: "This is the last Sunday."*
>
>*or I think it won't happen again, this is the last year.*

F) Before nouns used as adjectives:

1 – She is going to take guitar lessons.

2 – Chicken soup is good for a cold.

3 – They told me that I have turkey legs.

4 – I am going to school now.

5 – I will see you at lunch.

6 – Do you want to go <u>by car</u>, <u>by train</u> or <u>by bus</u>?

But, we can say: I am going to visit or to see <u>the school</u>.

Indefinite Article

We have already said that indefinite article "*a*" is used before a noun beginning with a consonant sound as: a man, a boy, a woman, a girl and before a noun beginning with a vowel sound: an eye, an orange, an apple or an <u>h</u>our, an <u>h</u>onest man, an <u>h</u>eir; all the underlined letters are silent.

Note that the indefinite article is also used when we refer to the nationality or when we talk about the profession.

1) Liz is not <u>an American</u>; she is <u>a Chinese</u>.

2) My friend is <u>a good lawyer</u>; he is not <u>an engineer</u>.

The indefinite article is also used when we mention units of measure, or time.

Examples:

1) We are going to buy <u>a pound</u> of bread.

Fritz-Meyer Sannon, PhD.

2) Will you please get me <u>a gallon</u> of oil?

3) I need <u>a kilo</u> of meat.

4) She works for 50 dollars <u>an hour</u>.

5) I don't see her, she comes once <u>a week</u>.

6) I will do it once <u>a month</u>.

New English Grammar for ESL Students

Exercises

Exercises A

Underline all the definite articles.

1 – A friend in need is a friend indeed.

2 – Queens EOC is one of the best schools in NY.

3 – I love the color green.

4 – Don't go there without my permission.

5 – You have the right to go.

6 – We know the way to Boca Chica.

7 – My friend is very sick today.

8 – The way to a man's heart is through is stomach.

9 – He is the best student here.

10 – The dog and the cat hit each other.

Exercises B

Fill in the blank with the indefinite article if necessary

1 -………… ice cream is very good.

2 -………….Brazil is a big country in South America.

3 -…………..boy and………….girl are good friends.

4 – My daughter will take………….guitar lessons.

5 – She loves………….coffee.

6 – My sister is…………..best in the family.

7 -…………….coffee of Columbia is………….best.

8 – My father bought……………..horse yesterday.

9 – I love……………….donkeys.

10 -…………….Port-au-Prince is the capital of Haiti.

11 -…………….chicken soup is good for cold.

Exercise C

<u>Underline the definite article once and the indefinite article twice</u>

1 – She remember the name of her teacher.

2 – The men are always wrong.

3 – We don't like the way she did that.

4 – An apple a day keeps the doctor away.

5 – My wife is very sick.

6 – She has a very good car.

7 – Children love to play in the backyard.

8 – My teacher is a very honest man.

9 – My uncle has an airplane.

10 – A friend in need is a friend indeed.

Exercise D

<u>Write the definite article where it is necessary</u>

1 -………..oil is very important.

2 -………..oil is too dirty.

3 – My friend…………..left………….home long time ago.

4 – Don't eat……………..ice cream.

5 – Why do we have to go to……………Panama?

6 - ………………water is very important to them.

7 -………………general of the army is leaving for Japan.

8 -……………..general Goltenberg is in……………hospital.

9 – My friend is……………last to leave……………city.

10 -………………president Clinton was a good president.

Exercise E

<u>Write the appropriate article before the underlined words</u>

1 – Will you come to…………..<u>party</u> tonight?

2 – Sarah bought……………<u>house</u> last week?

3 – I see him once……………<u>week</u>.

4 – She gets paid 25 dollars……………<u>hour</u>.

5 – ………………<u>way</u> to……………<u>man's</u> heart is through his stomach.

6 – She loves……………<u>book</u> she is reading now.

7 – Santa Claus will be in……………<u>city</u> tonight.

8 – My mother will cook……………<u>good</u> meal.

9 – Would you like to buy……………<u>soda</u> for me?

10 - ……………..<u>apple</u> a day keeps the doctor away.

Exercise F

<u>Write an indefinite article where it is necessary</u>

1 – We came to the game by ……….car.

2 – My car has………….big problem.

3 – Be patient, I will be back…………..hour.

4 – ……………..apple……….day keeps the doctor away.

5 – She said that she knew……………name of the boy.

6 – I don't have…………….time to go there.

7 -……………automobile there is yours, isn't it?

8 – She will buy……………dictionary as soon as possible.

9 – Let's make……………..deal.

10 – I want to make……………..phone call right now.

11 -…………….ice cream is very delicious.

Fritz-Meyer Sannon, PhD.

New English Grammar for ESL Students

Church of San Francisco
Quito, Ecuador

Fritz-Meyer Sannon, PhD.

Chapter 2

Nouns

Definition: A noun (from Latin nomen: name) is a word used to name a living creature, a thing, a place, or an idea. Ex. Man, woman, dog, snake, bird, table, chair, blackboard, Santo Domingo, Quito, Alaska, Brooklyn, minute, hour, truth, courage, etc.

Different Kinds of Nouns

There are different kinds of nouns:

Proper nouns: Refer to names of people, cities, countries, and specific places. All proper nouns start with capital letters. *Examples: John, Liz, Marta, Sonia, Antonio, Barbados, Cali, Santiago, Ponce, Cojutepeque, etc.*

Fritz-Meyer Sannon, PhD.

Common nouns: Refer to things (not people) that could be concrete or abstract. *Examples: Truck, chair, pencil, book, love, laziness, etc.*

Concrete nouns: Refer to thing that we can touch, we can see. *Examples: bag, bicycle, shirt, skirt, car, etc.*

Abstract nouns: Anything we can not see, we can not touch, we can not hear. *Examples: spirit, God, honesty, courage, love, etc.*

Count nouns: Applied to concrete things we can count one, two, three, four, etc. *Examples: table, chair, student, motorcycle, ship, boat, etc.*

Mass nouns or **Non count nouns:** Applied to things you can see and touch, but we can't count. *Examples: milk, water, money, time, air, coffee, etc.*

Compound Nouns: Are specific nouns formed with two or three words. *Examples: brother-in-law, sister-in-law, foster care, post office, maid of honor, vice-president, etc.*

Collective nouns: Refer to simple nouns with the idea of many, a group. *Examples: school, university, hospital, team, club, etc.*

Exercises

Exercise A

<u>In the following sentences, indicate after the underlined nouns what kind of noun they are.</u>

1 – <u>Sonia</u> (proper nouns) went to the store to buy <u>milk</u>. (mass nouns)

2 – <u>Santo Domingo</u> ( ) is a very beautiful <u>city</u>. ( ).

3 – My <u>grandmother</u> ( ) likes <u>bagels</u> ( ) and <u>tea</u>. ( ).

4 – My <u>mother-in-law</u> ( ) bought me <u>coffee</u>. ( )

5 – My English <u>teacher</u> ( ) is a nice <u>person</u>. ( )

6 – Quebec ( ) is one of the most beautiful cities in Canada. ( )

7 – Alexandra ( ) will go to Florida. ( ).

8 – Quito ( ) is as beautiful as Bogotá. ( )

9 – I always go to church ( ) on Sundays. ( )

10 – My teacher likes donkeys ( ) and horses. ( )

Exercise B

In the following sentences, underline the **abstract nouns** once, the **collective nouns** twice and the **mass nouns** three times.

1 – A cup of hot tea is very good in the morning.

2 – Mr. William's children don't like to go to church.

3 – Paul and Lucia belong to the same club.

4 – If you can't stand the heat, get out of the kitchen.

5 – Sometimes, love is blind.

6 – Quito is the capital of Ecuador and one of the most beautiful cities in South America.

7 – My son Richard does not like diet soda.

8 – Necessity knows no law.

9 – Waiter, give me two cups of coffee and two bagels.

10 – Some children love milk, some do not.

11 – Susan and Peter will go to the university tonight.

12 – We go to the same club on week-ends.

13 – Most children don't believe in ghosts.

14 – My mother-in-law never goes to church alone.

15 – Empty vessels make the most noise.

Plural of nouns

a) Most nouns form their plurals by putting (s) to the singular.

Fritz-Meyer Sannon, PhD.

Examples:

Cat – Cats	Dog – Dogs
Book – Books	Clock – Clocks
Pencil – Pencils	Pen – Pens
Table – Tables	Pupil – Pupils

b) If the noun ends in (y) and the (y) is preceded by a vowel, we can add (s) to the singular. However if the (y) is preceded by a consonant we have to change the (y) to (ies).

Examples:

Boy – Boys	Body – Bodies
Day – Days	Cavity – Cavities
Toy – Toys	City – Cities
Way – Ways	Penny – Pennies

c) Nouns ending in (f) or (fe) change (f) or (fe) to (ves) except roofs, chiefs.

Examples:

Wife – Wives

Thief – Thieves

Shelf - Shelves

Half – Halves

Wolf – Wolves

d) Nouns ending in (o) change the (o) to (eos) for the plural form. **Except**: piano, radio, soprano, stereo and video.

Examples:

Buffalo – Buffaloes	*Mango – Mangoes*
Domino – Dominoes	*Mosquito – Mosquitoes*
Embargo – Embargoes	*Potato – Potatoes*
Hero - Heroes	*Tomato – Tomatoes*

e) Nouns ending with "ch," "sh," "s," "ss," "x," "z" form their plural by adding (*es*) to the singular.

CH　　　　church – churches

	punch – punches
SH	dish – dishes
	brush – brushes
S	bus – buses
	gas – gases
SS	glass – glasses
	dress – dresses
X	tax – taxes
	box – boxes
Z	waltz – waltzes
	buzz – buzz(es)

Exercise

<u>Change each sentence from singular to plural</u>

1 – The Catholic Church is located on Main street in Boston.

Examples: The Catholic churches are located...

2 – We need the brush to finish the job.

3 – Give me the glass of milk instead.

4 – That is the dress I want to buy.

5 – In this case, there is no match.

6 – The Boxer is not supposed to give him that punch.

7 – My wife wants me to buy the box.

8 – Did you wash the dish?

9 – The glass is full.

10 – Do you like to go to class?

11 – What is the biggest church in Milwaukee?

12 – I don't like to pay the tax.

13 – Stop putting the dish on the dress.

14 – The bus in Chicago is too fast.

15 – We heard the buzz when we came.

f) Here are some nouns with irregular plural forms.

Fritz-Meyer Sannon, PhD.

Alumna – Alumnae	*Fish – Fish*
Analysis – Analyses	*Foot – Feet*
Appendix – Appendices	*Louse – Lice*
Bacterium – Bacteria	*Man – Men*
Child – Children	*Means – Means*
Criterion – Criteria	*Mouse – Mice*
Curriculum – Curricula	*Ox – Oxen*
Datum – Data	*Series – Series*
Deer – Deer	*Woman – Women*

Exercise A

<u>Change each of the following sentences from singular to plural</u>

1 – The cat in the living room is heavy.

2 – The city never sleeps.

3 – A large buffalo was in my backyard yesterday.

4 – There was a big mosquito in my soup.

5 – A tomato a day keeps the doctor away.

6 – My daughter eats a potato and a tomato for lunch.

7 – We need a good stereo in the living room.

8 – My brother loves his radio.

9 – There is not a borough in the big city.

10 – There is only one hero in town.

Exercise B

<u>Change the following to plural forms</u>

1 – The alumna didn't pay her due last year.

2 – What is the criterion for judging the parts?

3 – The candidate brings the curriculum to the adviser.

4 – She has a penny in her purse.

5 – It seems that the horse in my bedroom is dead.

6 – There is a series of good fiction books.

7 – The man over there catches one big fish.

8 – There was a baby deer in the backyard this morning.

Fritz-Meyer Sannon, PhD.

9 – How much is the baby sheep?

10 – The wolf walks alone in the park.

Homonyms

Definition: (From Greek Homo = same and Onyma or Onoma = name) a word pronounced like another, but different in meaning and in spelling. *Examples: Piece, peace; sea, see; two, too, to; feat, feet; etc.*

Homographs

Definition: they are also homonyms except that the spelling are the same.

Examples:

Present (gift)	*Raise (to elevate, to build)*
Present (v. to present)	*Raise (increase in amount)*
Principal (adj. main)	*Since (preposition)*
Principal (person with authority)	*Since (conjunction)*

Homophones

Definition: They are also homonyms, they have the same sound, and the spellings are different. ***Examples: Blew, blue; piece, peace; to, two, too; sea, see; sew, saw, so are*** **called homonyms and homophones.**

Synonyms

Definition: One, two or three words having the same or about the same meaning. ***Bright, sharp, and intelligent*** **have about the same meaning.**

Here are some common synonyms:

Accidental – casual – contingent

Achieve – accomplish – acquire

Adequate – enough – satisfactory

Ambition – aspiration – goal

Common – familiar – frequent

Close – shut – stop

Fritz-Meyer Sannon, PhD.

Effective – efficient

Fool – idiot – imbecile

Slay – kill

Tough – hard – firm

Tranquil – calm – quiet

Transparent – clear – limpid

Antonyms

Definition: A word which is opposite in meaning to another word.

Examples: Old is the antonym of new or young

Ugly – beautiful

Strong – weak

Here are some antonyms:

Brave – cowardly	*Stop – begin, start*
Dirty – clean	*Tough – frail, fragile*
Large – little, small, tiny	*Truth – lie*

Natural – artificial   *Valid – void, null*

Normal – bizarre, odd   *Wait – leave*

Rich – poor   *War – peace*

Stable – variable   *Wet – dry*

Fritz-Meyer Sannon, PhD.

Exercises

Exercise A

In each of the following sentences there is one word which is an incorrect homonym. Please write the correct homonyn.

1 – Some people like piece; they don't like war.

2 – It takes too to tango.

3 – My father said, "Wear there is a will, there is a way!"

4 – Dolores sew the teacher yesterday.

5 – Although I am diabetic, I sometimes take a peace of cake.

6 – We want to by a house next year.

7 – This man has good principals.

8 – She leaves on main street with her mom.

9 – On her birthday, she herself blue out the candles.

10 – Sarita wants to bee a good nurse.

11 – My grandmother is very seek.

Exercise B

Substitute the underlined word with a synonym

1 – Peter and Sonia are the smartest students in this class.

2 – The robbers slay the security guard and run away.

3 – This is a very effective measure he took.

4 – The examiner thinks this is not adequate to get the job.

5 – Professor Fritz always shuts the door when class is in session.

6 – I think this is an insult not to answer my letter.

7 – My nephew has a lot of ambitions.

8 – The teachers at Queens EOC are very capable.

9 – Mr. Williams and Mrs. Lee work vigorously.

10 – Kharriyah is a very sharp person.

11 – Almost all languages from the western world have about the same syntactic structure.

12 – Some people here are very rude.

Fritz-Meyer Sannon, PhD.

Exercises C

Substitute the underlined word with an antonyms

1 – Our English class <u>stops</u> at 6:00 o'clock.

2 – The document is <u>valid</u> until the expiration date.

3 – California is as <u>small</u> as New York.

4 – Computer language is a <u>natural</u> language.

5 – Brasilia is a very <u>old</u> city in Brazil.

6 – Santiago is <u>smaller</u> than Havana.

7 – The <u>first</u> time she saw Paris, her heart was <u>cold</u> and gay.

8 – Better a live coward than a <u>live</u> hero.

9 – Beauty is in the eyes of the beholder; sometimes, <u>hate</u> is blind.

10 – I do not like this wrestler, he is too <u>brave</u>.

11 – We do not want to wait <u>before</u> time passes.

12 – There are a lot of <u>rich</u> and <u>healthy</u> people in this neighborhood.

13 – The way to a <u>woman's</u> heart is through <u>her</u> stomach.

14 – After fall comes winter; <u>after</u> summer comes spring.

Possessive case

Sometimes the complement of the noun is placed before the noun or pronoun denoting ownership: *Peter's car or the car of Peter.*

1 – The possessive case is formed by adding (') and (**s**) to <u>singular or plural</u> nouns not ending in (**s**) or (**z**).

Examples: *Man's suit* *Men's suits*

2 – The possessive case is formed by adding (') to singular nouns of one syllable even those ending by (**s**) or (**z**).

Examples: *The boss's* *Charles's motocycle*

3 – The possessive case is formed by adding (') without (**s**) to singular nouns of more than one syllable ending in (**s**) or (**z**).

Examples: *Politeness' rule* *Goodness' sake*

Fritz-Meyer Sannon, PhD.

4 – The possessive case is formed by adding (') without **(s)** to plural nouns ending in **(s) or (z)**.

Examples: The churches' doors   Dishes' colors

Exercise

Use the possessive case if necessary

1 – The dress of Lucia.

2 – The bags of the women.

3 – I love the office of my grandfather.

4 – Those are the suitcases of the men.

5 – The house of my mother is new.

6 – Go and see the room of my boss.

7 – The motorcycle of Charles is fast.

8 – I like to see the room of the children.

9 – We admire the colors of the dishes.

10 – Thank you for giving me the picture of Cruz.

11 – Mom always touches the doors of the churches.

12 – They look like the tails of the foxes.

13 – That is the white car of Carlos.

14 – Thank you for giving me the book of Mercedes.

15 – For the sake of goodness, I am free.

Fritz-Meyer Sannon, PhD.

New English Grammar for ESL Students

Indian Procession Fiesta of
Nuestra Senora de los Angeles, Guatemala

Fritz-Meyer Sannon, PhD.

Chapter 3

Adjectives

Definition: (From Latin Adjicere, to add to) is a word used to describe or modify a noun or a pronoun. It is also used to specify a thing as distinct from something else.

Example: <u>Big</u> house, <u>beautiful</u> garden, <u>tall</u> building, <u>red</u> flower, <u>dirty</u> boy, <u>slow</u> car.

Different Kinds of Adjectives:

Kinds of Adjectives: There are about eight different kinds of adjectives.

Fritz-Meyer Sannon, PhD.

1 – **Descriptive adjectives:** Those adjectives added to the words to identify, to qualify, to distinguish, to give the essential nature of the words.

Examples: White horse   *Blue ink*

Beautiful house   *Ugly girl*

Green car   *Fat lady*

Smart student   *Stupid man*

2 – **Proper adjectives:** are adjectives derived from a proper noun.

Examples: Cesarean surgery   *Shakespearean tragedy*

Stalinist method   *Freudian philosophy*

Marxist theory   *Platonic love*

3 – **Possessive adjectives:** The person or people to whom an object, thing or idea belongs.

The possessive adjectives are for singular and plural.

My

Your

His, her, its

Our

Your

Their

Examples: **My** book is on the table.

Your homework is on the teacher's desk.

His car is blue and white. (Masculine)

Her dress is too long. (Feminine)

The white cat moves **its** tail.

Our teacher is very quiet today.

Your toys are dirty.

Their shoes are new.

4 – **Demonstrative adjectives**: Used to show or specify people, things, ideas that are distinct from others.

Fritz-Meyer Sannon, PhD.

The demonstrative adjectives for singular: **This, that**

For plural: **These, those**

Example: *The dictionary is very expensive.* (**This** is for something close to the speaker.)

That dictionary is very expensive. (**That** is for something far from the speaker.)

These books on my desk are new. (**For** things near the speaker)

Those books over there are new. (**Far** from the speaker)

5 – **Numeral cardinal adjectives:** Used in simple counting to express and represent numbers, like *one, two, three, four, forty, sixty,* etc.

*Examples: There are more than **ninety** pigeons on the sidewalk.*

*I have **seven** dollars in my pocket.*

Two *dogs walk together.*

*Will you please give me **one** cup of coffee and **three** bagels.*

6 – **Numeral ordinal adjectives:** Usually used to indicate order, succession: **First, second, third.**

*Examples: There is a French-Spanish bookstore on **Fifth Avenue**.*

*On **Second Avenue** in Manhattan, New York, there are many boutiques.*

*Believe it or not, the new mayor did a good job on **Forty-second Street**.*

*July **fourth** is a special day for American people.*

*Macy's is one of the best department stores. In New York the main store is located on **Thirty-fourth Street** between **sixth** and **Seventh Avenue**.*

7 – **Interrogative adjectives:** Are question words **always** placed before nouns, when asking questions: *what, which, whose,* etc.

Fritz-Meyer Sannon, PhD.

Examples: <u>*What*</u> *time is it now?*

<u>*What*</u> *train goes to Brooklyn?*

<u>*Which*</u> *train runs at this time?*

<u>*Whose*</u> *book is that?*

<u>*Which*</u> *house is yours?*

<u>*Whose*</u> *car is the blue car?*

8 – **Indefinite adjectives:** such adjectives do not define exactly the range or the limit*: some, every*, etc.

Examples: <u>*Some*</u> *people think they know everything.*

<u>*Any*</u> *student is free to go.*

<u>*Many*</u> *students will do their homework.*

<u>*Much*</u> *sugar and* <u>*much*</u> *milk.*

<u>*Each*</u> *star represents a state.*

Note 1: All the adjectives mentioned are placed before the nouns they modify. Sometimes adjectives are used as nouns.

*Example 1. The **rich** Dominican gives 2,000 dollars to the **poor** man.*

In the sentence above **rich** and **poor** modify Dominican and man.

*The **rich** don't pay attention to the **poor**.*

In that sentence, **rich** and **poor** are nouns, not adjectives.

Example 2. *That **old** lady walks slowly.*

Old is an adjective.

*We have to protect the **old** and the **young**.*

Both **old** and **young** are used as nouns.

Note 2: Sometimes one of two words next to each other (not compound nouns) could be used as adjective; the first describes the other.

Examples: Apple pie	*Garden flower*
Body language	*Retirement money*
Boat people	*Vacation house*

Fritz-Meyer Sannon, PhD.

Car radio   *Wedding dress*

- When she talks, she uses <u>body language</u>.

- My father brought me a <u>car radio</u>.

- I don't have anything to bring to grandma; I will bring her my <u>garden flowers</u>.

- I will use my <u>retirement money</u> to buy a condo.

Exercises

Exercise A

<u>Underline the descriptive adjectives in the following sentences</u>

1 – Children are very happy when they play.

2 – Yesterday was a very hot day.

3 – Everyday is a good day.

4 – Why do you think that woman is so sad?

5 – My sister has a tough job.

6 – George is a very young fellow.

7 – Happiness is a good thing; unhappy people are miserable.

8 – Like my mother, I love garden flowers.

9 – Tell me how old you are.

10 – The soldiers are very courageous.

Exercise B

Underline once all the demonstrative and twice all the possessive adjectives

1 – Those students make too much noise.

2 – This big car is my father's.

3 – Where are you going at this time?

4 – I love this house.

5 – My uncle said that he was tired?

6 – I love her very much.

7 – Its tail is too long.

8 – Their house is too old.

9 – The telephone that I bought is terrific.

10 – Our school is very clean.

Exercise C

Underline the interrogative adjectives in the following sentences

1 – Who are you?

2 – Which shirts do you want to buy?

3 – What time is it?

4 – Could you state which one is hers?

5 – I don't know what you mean.

6 – Whose bicycle do you want to buy?

7 – Which car is yours?

8 – What book do you want?

9 – Could you tell me which car is yours?

10 – What day is today?

Exercise D

Circle each of the indefinite adjectives (if any) in the following sentences

1 – I drink a lot of water in summer.

2 – Somebody came last night and asked for you.

3 – Some want to go to the park.

4 – How much is each?

5 – Someone has to take the responsibility.

6 – Some people are responsible, some are not.

7 – I don't have any money with me.

8 – Every man has the same chance.

9 – Everybody has the same chance.

10 – I buy many toys during summertime for my son.

11 – Each day brings a new surprise.

12 – Everyone is free to go.

Fritz-Meyer Sannon, PhD.

Exercise E

Put (nc) above the numeral cardinal adjective and (no) above the numeral ordinal

1 – Let's go to Fifth avenue with me.

2 – I would like to buy five suits.

3 – Six and six are twelve.

4 – My son-in-law won two million dollars.

5 – World War Two ended in nineteen forty-five.

6 – My first wife died five years ago.

7 – My first trip this year will be in Africa.

8 – My grandmother is ninety years old.

9 – There are more than two hundred seventy million people in the USA.

10 – Pick me up and I will give you two dollars.

11 – I like to go to Fifth avenue on Saturdays.

12 – My brother went to Milwaukee and bought three pairs of shoes.

Adjectives and Degrees

There are three degrees in adjectives.

a) Positive   **b) Comparative**   **c) Superlative**

Examples of positive degree:

good, hard, smart, cheap, expensive.

Comparative degree: We use the comparative when we compare two (not more than two) *things, people, ideas*, etc.

Comparative of superiority: We form the comparative of superiority by adding **(er)** to the positive degree, if the adjective has one or two syllables.

*Examples: Pierre is **taller** than his brother.*

*Lucia is **shorter** than her mother.*

*This suit is **cheaper** than that one.*

If the adjective ends in (y) we must change (y) to (ier).

Fritz-Meyer Sannon, PhD.

Example: *This lesson is **easier** than the last lesson.*

*People who live here are **happier** than those who live over there.*

What about if the adjective has more than two syllables:

Comfortable, expensive, convenient, difficult.

If the adjective has more than two syllables, we must use **"more"** before the positive degree.

*Examples: Taxis are **more expensive** than trains.*

*Taxis are also **more comfortable** than trains.*

*This lesson is **more difficult** than the last one.*

*This room is **more convenient** for the party than the green room.*

Remark: It is necessary and even obligatory to use **"than"** after the comparative form.

Comparative of equality: *"As...as"* the comparative of equality is used when we compare two persons, two of equal value.

Pierre is **as tall as** his brother.

Lucia is **as short as** her mother.

This suit is **as cheap as** that one.

This lesson is **as difficult as** the previous one.

This room is **as convenient as** the green room.

Comparative of inferiority: *"less...than"*

We use the comparative of inferiority when we compare two persons, two things of unequal value:

Examples: 1 – Pierre is **less tall** than his brother.

2 – Lucia is **less short** than her mother.

3 – This suit is **less cheap** *than that one.*

4 – This chapter twelve is **less difficult** *than the chapter eleven.*

Fritz-Meyer Sannon, PhD.

5 – This room is **<u>less convenient</u>** than the green room.

Some adjectives have special forms for the comparative.

Good – better   ill – worse

Bad – worse   Much – more

Far – farther, further   etc.

Examples: This method is very good.

- This method is better than the old one.

- That student is smart.

- That student is smarter than his friend.

- Chicago is farther than Washington, D.C. from here.

Superlative: We form the superlative by adding (**est**) to the positive degree. We use the superlative when we compare more than two.

Positive	**Comparative**	**Superlative**
Tall	Taller	Tallest
Short	Shorter	Shortest

Long	*Longer*	*Longest*
Cheap	*Cheaper*	*Cheapest*
Easy	*Easier*	*Easiest*

If the adjective has more than two syllables, we add **"the most"** to the positive degree.

Examples:

<u>Positive</u>	<u>Comparative</u>	<u>Superlative</u>
Convenient	*More convenient*	*The most convenient*
Difficult	*More difficult*	*The most difficult*
Expensive	*More expensive*	*The most expensive*
Comfortable	*More comfortable*	*The most comfortable*
Intelligent	*More intelligent*	*The most intelligent*

Fritz-Meyer Sannon, PhD.

Exercises

Exercise A

Change the word in parentheses to the comparative form of superiority

1 – Water is (good) than soda.

2 – Tom is (short) …………………his cousin.

3 – My car (fast)…………………yours.

4 – Santo Domingo is a great deal (beautiful)………………..Higuey.

5 – Eduardo is always (serious)……………………Jose.

6 – New Jersey is (near) from here.

7 – This class is (busy)…………………that class.

8 – New York City is (large) than Newark.

9 – The weather is (warm) today…………………yesterday.

10 – The teacher is (old)…………………Miguel.

11 – This student has (much) money………………..we do.

12 – Taxis are (comfortable)………………trains.

13 – My aunt has (expensive) furniture………………..we do.

14 – This car is (expensive)………………….that car.

15 – New York City is (big)………………….Chicago.

Exercise B

Complete and change to the comparative form of equality

1 – This train is fast

Example: This train is as fast as the bus.

2 – This one is old…

3 – I am big…

4 – Toronto is clean…

5 – Illinois is noisy…

6 – That house is small…

7 – Carlos is serious…

8 – Quito is beautiful…

9 – Brooklyn is large…

10 – That man is tall…

11 – The boys and girls are young…

12 – My cousin is very pretty…

13 – Bogota is beautiful…

14 – Broadway is wide…

Exercise C

Complete and make comparisons of inferiority with the adjectives in parentheses

1 – Alicia is (short)…

Example: Alicia is less short than Tania.

2 – New Jersey is (big)…

3 – Montreal is (large)…

4 – Amy is (bright)…

5 – Tom's house is (small)…

7 – Do you think this is (difficult)…

8 – This exercise looks (easy)…

9 – That man is (polite)…

10 – Josefina is (pretty)……………Margarita.

11 – The weather today is (good)…

12 – Tony is (popular)…

13 – Orange is (sweet)…

Exercise D

Change the following to superlative form

1 – Carlos writes (good) papers of all.

Example: Carlos writes the best papers of all.

2 – That's (comfortable) chair in this room.

3 – My mother is (nice) person in the family.

4 – Concorde is (fast) plane in the world.

5 – Brazil is (big) country in South America.

6 – International University is (interesting) modern institution of all.

7 – Princeton is one (good) school in Philadelphia.

8 – Pace University is (small) university in New York.

9 – Michelle is (friendly) girl in this office.

10 – Columbia is (beautiful) country in South America.

11 – My son is (reserved) in the family.

12 – Her daughter is (timid) girl in the neighborhood.

13 – Carlos is (old) man in the class.

14 – My room is (attractive) in this house.

15 – That lesson is (easy) of all.

New English Grammar for ESL Students

An ESL student's backyard in Chaloitenango,
(El Salvador)

Fritz-Meyer Sannon, PhD.

Chapter 4

Pronouns

Definition: (From Latin Pronomen, pro + nomen, name) A pronoun is a word used in place of a noun mentioned elsewhere.

Different Kinds of Pronouns:

There are different kinds of pronouns:

Personal pronouns: (Subject and object)

Example: he, him

Demonstrative pronouns: *(This, that, these, those)*

Possessive pronouns: *(Yours, hers, ours)*

Interrogative pronouns: *(Who, what, which)*

Indefinite pronouns: *(Everyone, somebody)*

Relative pronouns: *(Who, which, that, etc.)*

Fritz-Meyer Sannon, PhD.

Reflexive pronouns: *(Himself, herself, etc.)*

Intensive pronouns: *(Myself, ourselves, etc.)*

Reciprocal pronouns: (Each other, one another)

Note: A singular pronoun refers to a singular noun; while a plural pronoun refers to a plural noun.

Personal pronouns:

Personal pronoun subjects are:

I, you, he, she, it, we, you, they. The personal pronouns subjects are asked when we indicate that the person, or the animal does the action or makes the statement.

Examples: Paul went to Camaguey; <u>he</u> *bought a blue shirt.* <u>He</u> is the personal pronoun subject, he (replacing Paul, did the action of buying a shirt.

Susan and Franco were in San Salvador; <u>they</u> *visited the museum.* "They" replaces Susan and Franco, personal pronouns subject because they did the action of visiting.

Personal pronouns object are:

Me, you, him, her, it, you, them. The personal pronouns object are used when we indicate the person, or the animal, the action is referred to.

*Examples: We love Andrea. We love **her**.* Andrea does not do any action. **She** is not the subject. She is the object of the verb to love.

We kill the mouse. We kill it. "**It**" is a personal pronoun object, "it" replaces mouse. The mouse does not do any action. We do the action of killing. Mouse is complement; "**it**" (replacing mouse) is the object of the verb to kill.

Demonstrative pronouns are:

This, that (singular) these, those (plural) the demonstrative pronouns have the same form as the demonstrative adjectives. But, the demonstrative pronouns are not determinative like articles or adjectives. They are pronouns; they take the place of nouns.

*Examples: I saw the **crowd**. I saw **that**.* "That" replaces the crowd, it is a pronoun, it is a demonstrative pronoun.

That *crowd is big.* "**That**", placed before a noun does not replace crowd, it determines crowd; it is an adjective. Demonstrative pronouns are used when we point to something already mentioned.

For instance:

Did you see the flowers there? Yes, I saw those. Those is a pronoun, a demonstrative pronoun.

Possessive pronouns are:

Mine, yours, his, hers, its, ours, yours, theirs. Possessive pronouns are usually used when we indicate that something belongs to a person, an animal, or a thing.

Examples: This beautiful house is my house. Instead of using house twice, we use a word to replace house: This beautiful house is **mine**. "**Mine**" is a possessive pronoun.

The car over there is your car. It is not necessary to repeat car a second time. Instead, the car over there is **yours**. "**Yours**" is a possessive pronoun.

The dirty shirt in the closet is his shirt. We do not have to repeat shirt twice; there is a pronoun we can use in place of shirt. The shirt in the closet is **"his"**.

The hat on the dining room table is her hat. The word hat does not have to appear twice in the same sentence. We could use a word that replaces the word hat. Instead of saying: The **hat** on the dining room table is her hat; Say, The **hat** on the dining room table is **hers**. "**Hers**" is a possessive pronoun. Please do not confuse possessive adjectives and possessive pronouns. Adjectives are determinative and pronouns are not determinative; pronouns are subjects and objects.

Example: His car is very old. Here **"his"** is an adjective. The old car is **"his"**. Here, **"his"** is a pronoun.

<u>Interrogative pronouns</u> are:

Who, whom, whose, what, which. When do we use interrogative pronouns?

When we interrogate, when we use a sentence expressing, containing, or implying a question.

Examples: Who are you?

Whom do you want to speak to?

Whose are they?

What is your real name?

Which do you think it refers to?

Those are question words usually placed at the beginning of a sentence when we make a question.

Note that the pronoun replaces a noun.

Pronouns are never determinative. See the difference between:

a) "**What**" time is it?

b) "**What**" is your name?

In (a) "**what**" does not replace a noun, "**what**" determines the noun time. In other words, every time it is placed before a noun, it is an adjective. In (b) "**what**" is a pronoun. The pronoun is either a subject or an object. Pronouns never determine.

Examples: *"**Which**" table do you want?* (adjective)

*"**Which**" is the best way to go to Brooklyn?* (pronoun)

a) ***What** was the real price?* (pronoun)

b) ***What** price is this?* (adjective)

Remark: "Who" **is always a pronoun, never an adjective.**

Fritz-Meyer Sannon, PhD.

Example: Who are you?

Who came last night?

Who wants to be a millionaire?

We cannot say *Who time is it? Or *Who student is he?

Indefinite pronouns are:

Somebody, someone, anybody, anything, no one, something, somewhat, everything, everybody, etc. Indefinite implies something vague, not specified. Indefinite pronouns refer to people or things not definite. Indefinite pronouns are sometimes singular, or plural; however, in informal English (not in standard English) they use possessive plural form (their in place of his or her) to refer to indefinite pronoun.

Examples: Someone took his bag from the locker. (SAE) Standard American English vs.

Someone took their bag from the locker. (informal)

Everyone in this class has the right to go there to pick up his price. (formal)

v.s

Everyone in this class has the right to go there to pick up their price. (informal)

Like the other pronouns, the indefinite pronouns are always subjects or objects.

Here are some examples:

- **_Someone_** had to do it.

- **_No one_** entered the room last night.

- **_Everybody_** loves somebody sometimes.

- **_Somebody_** was here because the light is on.

- **_Everyone_** has the same right in this house.

- **_Nothing_** is perfect on earth.

- **_Somebody_** followed me yesterday.

- **_Nobody_** should sit on this chair.

Fritz-Meyer Sannon, PhD.

- **_Many_** *went to the party.*

Compare: **"many"** students go to the museum this summer.

(adj) **"Many"** go to the museum, this summer.

Relative pronouns are:

Who, whom, whose, that, which. Relative pronouns refer back to nouns or pronouns and also connect a subordinate clause.

Here are some examples:

*1 – The girl **who** was here yesterday is my daughter.*

*2 – The old man **who** came in the office is Dr. Ruth's patient.*

*3 – The man **whom** I always speak to is a star.*

*4 – The lady **that** bought the car had a lot of money.*

*5 – Don't tell me that the man **whose** car is here is blind.*

*6 – The movie **which** we saw last night was scary.*

*7 – Here are the **books that** you are looking for.*

8 – The student **that** *brings the dog in the class is impolite.*

The <u>relative pronoun</u> always introduce a subordinate clause, also called relative clause because the clause is started by a relative pronoun. Please remember **"that"** could be a demonstrative adjective (chapter 3). **"That"** man is sleeping. **That** could be a demonstrative pronoun. I want to buy **"that"**. **That** could be a conjunction (see chapter 13). I know **"that"** you don't like me. **That** finally could be a relative pronoun when it refers back to a noun placed next to and when it introduces a subordinate clause.

Examples: The boys ***that*** *arrived late are twins.*

The books ***that*** *are on the desk are mine.*

<u>Reflexive pronouns</u> are:

Myself, yourself, himself, herself, itself, ourselves, yourselves, themselves.

Fritz-Meyer Sannon, PhD.

The reflexive pronoun refers to the person who does the action or directs the action back to the doer or subject. In other words, the same person does the action and receives the action.

Examples: Yolanda cuts herself.

- Mr. Roger shaves himself every morning.

- The soldiers killed themselves.

- We look at ourselves in the mirror.

- In the first sentence:

- Yolanda cuts herself.

The subject is **Yolanda**; the verb is **cuts** and the object is **herself** which is a pronoun replacing **Yolanda**. In this case, **Yolanda** is the subject and **Yolanda** is the object. **Yolanda cuts Yolanda or Yolanda cuts herself.**

Intensive pronouns are:

Myself, yourself, himself, herself, ourselves, yourselves, themselves.

Intensive pronouns have the same forms like the reflexive pronouns. The difference is the reflexive pronoun refers back to the subject, to the doer as in:

Juana cuts herself.

In this example Juana cuts Juana.

Juana herself cuts the bread.

The subject is **Juana** but the object is not Juana; the object is **bread**.

Juana cuts what? The bread.

Herself placed after Juana emphasizes the preceding noun. Juana **"herself"** (nobody else) cuts the bread. In this example, **herself** which is placed next to the subject is not a reflexive pronoun; it is an intensive pronoun.

By the way, don't confuse the expressions: **"by myself"**, **"by yourself", or "by himself"** with reflexive or intensive pronouns. They are strictly idiomatic expressions meaning "alone"

Here are some examples:

- *Juan goes to work everyday **by himself**.*

- *Juan goes to work everyday alone.*

- *The two sisters go to the beach **by themselves**.*

- *The two sisters go to the beach alone.*

- *I like to go to the movies **by myself**.*

- *I like to go to the movies alone.*

Reciprocal pronouns are:

Each other, one another. We use the reciprocal pronouns when we refer to people or things related to each other. One completes the other. *"Each other"* is used when we refer to two persons; *"one another"* is used when we refer to more than two persons.

Here are some examples:

1 – Luis and Maria look at **each other**.

2 – Antonia and Robert kiss **each other**.

3 – The cat and the dog hit **each other**.

4 – The Palestinians and the Israelis kill **one another**.

5 – The girls and the boys bite **one another**.

Fritz-Meyer Sannon, PhD.

Exercises

Exercise A

<u>Underline the personal pronouns</u>

1 – Martha goes to school. She likes the school.

2 – He loves his mother.

3 – My mother lives in Connecticut. She loves me.

4 – They are busy and they can't wait for him.

5 – My uncle is old; he is very rich.

6 – We pick her up every day.

7 – They love football.

8 – It is on the table.

9 – My sister likes basketball. She goes to college.

10 – They went to Chicago with him.

Exercise B

Underline the personal pronoun object

1 – Look at the sky; <u>it</u> is not blue today.

2 – My sister saw <u>him</u> yesterday.

3 – We love <u>them</u>.

4 – You don't want <u>them</u>.

5 – Give <u>us</u> a chance.

6 – They saw <u>us</u> yesterday.

7 – I gave <u>you</u> my word.

8 – The girls see <u>them</u>.

9 – We told <u>her</u> to return.

10 – She ate French fries.

11 – The birds eat in my backyard.

12 – My friend is angry.

13 – I don't like <u>them</u>.

14 – I gave <u>him</u> 2 dollars.

Fritz-Meyer Sannon, PhD.

Exercise C

Write (PS) after the personal pronoun subject and (PO) after the personal pronoun object

1 – Who are they?

2 – We went to Yankee stadium last week. It's so beautiful.

3 – She likes the school.

4 – Dr. Gordon is very nice. She takes care of everybody.

5 – Goodbye, guys, I will see you later.

6 – Anna wants to repeat the class; she loves it.

7 – Mrs. Lateef is a nice person too. I don't like to talk about her.

8 – Martha and I will get married.

9 – My mother does not like him.

10 – We gave you too much money.

11 – Don't worry, I don't like him.

12 – Give it to me.

13 – We love her very much.

14 – She is my best friend.

15 – Maria is nice, but she is too shy.

Exercise D

<u>Underline all the relative pronouns</u>

1 – The truck which is over there is out of service.

2 – Who was the guy that was singing here?

3 – Those who come late won't get anything.

4 – The man whose bicycle is in the backyard is a police officer.

5 – Which car do you like?

6 – The lady who bought my house is a millionaire.

7 – Who is going over there?

8 – I don't like the shoes which you bought.

9 – My mother had a big old car which I didn't like.

10 – The dog that is sleeping over there is hers.

11 – Many people who came yesterday were not interested.

12 – The boy who was here had an accident.

Exercise E

<u>Replace the incorrect relative pronouns by the correct ones</u>

1 – The boy which goes there is stupid.

2 – Don't buy something which you don't like.

3 – Don't go to the river.

4 – She likes the shirt which she bought.

5 – The gentlemen whose I spoke to were very polite.

6 – Take the book who is on the table for me.

7 – I want to see it now.

8 – The cat who stands there was absent yesterday.

9 – Hartford which is the capital of Connecticut is a beautiful city.

10 – Which of the town is New Canaan?

11 – Ivory Coast which is one of the French speaking countries has many intellectuals.

12 – They want to buy a house which is in Bridgeport.

13 – Every time I see my son who is here, I feel proud.

14 – Give me a piece that I could eat.

15 – The woman who I saw yesterday is my neighbor.

Exercise F

Underline the possessive pronoun in the following sentences

1 – My cousin wanted to buy this.

2 – Get one of his.

3 – She likes mine.

4 – We like hers.

5 – Love it or leave it.

6 – The doctor has his office in Queens.

7 – My car is dirty.

8 – She doesn't like mine.

9 – Maria likes mine.

10 – We take our money, she takes hers.

11 – Give me your book.

12 – Listen, let me see yours.

13 – I don't want to buy his.

14 – My mother does not like yours.

15 – We don't like theirs.

Exercise G

Underline the demonstrative pronouns

1 – Silvia bought that a long time ago.

2 – If I were you, I would do it.

3 – Do you think she appreciates that?

4 – This class is too small.

5 – My wife took those to the boutique.

6 – I like this.

7 – Marie doesn't like those.

8 – Did you buy those flowers?

9 – Give me that.

10 – How come you take those?

11 – My friend didn't like those.

12 – That man is very poor.

Exercise H

Put (DA) after demonstrative adjectives and (DP) after the demonstrative pronouns

1 – Those flowers do not smell good.

2 – Those toys belong to my grandson.

3 – That chair is made of iron.

4 – She wants to keep this.

5 – Those trees are very big.

6 – Those things mean a lot to me.

7 – She did receive those.

8 – I don't like that.

9 – This building has 102 stories.

10 – That man is really crazy.

11 – Those students don't understand anything.

12 – That table has three legs.

13 – I don't appreciate that.

14 – These trees look like mango trees.

Exercise I

Underline all personal pronouns (sub. and object) and put a checkmark after the demonstrative pronouns

1 – She put the car in the garage.

2 – I like him.

3 – Three and three are six.

4 – If you like me, give me that.

5 – She wakes up at 7 o'clock every morning.

6 – My dog was a baby.

7 – That house is too old.

8 – I don't love her.

9 – I really like that.

10 – Maria doesn't believe she did that.

11 – We love those.

12 – Today is her birthday.

13 – My friend has a big car.

14 – We understand her situation.

Exercise J

Put (PA) after the possessive adjective, (PP) after the possessive pronouns, (DA) after demonstrative adjectives

1 – Our town is beautiful.

2 – Her hair is long.

3 – If you go there, I will stay here.

4 – Our parents are very old.

5 – We don't have the courage to take our responsibilities.

6 – She has her way of doing it.

7 – Their room is empty.

8 – My house and her house are next to each other.

9 – That bicycle is his.

10 – Give me your pencil.

11 – My friend has her own bicycle.

12 – His book is new.

13 – That car over there is hers.

14 – His house is too big.

Exercise K

Underline the intensive pronouns

1 – I myself play in the backyard with Grandpa.

2 – We ourselves change the flag.

3 – Leclerc, Bonaparte's brother-in-law, himself spoke to Toussaint Louverture.

4 – I hate to go to the movies of myself.

5 – That man does not like himself.

6 – Ella did not plan to go there by herself.

7 – We ourselves invade the small island.

8 – We don't like it all.

9 – Noriega himself went to buy weapons.

10 – She goes to buy bread herself.

11 – My parents themselves clean the house.

12 – She herself bought a good car.

Exercise L

Underline all the reflexive pronouns

1 – She knows herself very well.

3 – We shave ourselves everyday.

4 – The baby bites herself.

5 – Go to the movie yourself.

6 – We don't know anything.

7 – My wife hurt herself.

8 – My father cut himself.

9 – We do it ourselves.

10 – I look at myself in the mirror.

Exercise M

Indicate by (RP) all reflexive pronouns; by (IP) all intensive pronouns

1 – I myself shave my father.

2 – I cut myself with a big knife.

3 – She shaves herself.

4 – We look at ourselves in the mirror.

5 – She herself prepares the dinner.

6 – Don't go there; take care of yourself.

7 – We ourselves fix the car.

8 – I myself bought the refrigerator.

9 – They themselves cut the trees.

10 – She herself painted the whole room.

11 – I like myself.

12 – She herself cooked for Thanksgiving.

13 – My aunt hit herself.

Exercise N

Underline the reciprocal pronoun

1 – Haitian brothers kill one another.

2 – Give me that.

3 – Suzie and Kevin love each other.

4 – Dominicans and Haitians dislike one another.

5 – She doesn't like to look at herself in the mirror.

6 – Brothers and sisters always hit one another.

7 – I myself see the cow.

8 – Maria and Pedro love each other.

9 – You and I love each other.

10 – The two sisters hate each other.

11 – They looked at one another this morning.

12 – The brothers bite each other.

13 – The prisoners hit one another.

14 – The Israelis and the Palestinians kill one another.

Exercise O

<u>Underline all the interrogative adjectives</u>

1 – Which train do you take after school?

2 – When is payday?

3 – What day will we get the bonus?

4 – Which is my room?

5 – What time is it?

6 – What is your name?

7 – This house is beautiful.

8 – That car is not mine?

9 – Whose shoes are those?

10 – Who are you?

11 – Which room do you want to stay in?

12 – Who was in the basement today?

Exercise P

Indicate by a checkmark all the interrogative pronouns

1 – Who are you?

2 – Since you are so polite, I give you a ticket to go to Radio City.

3 – Before you came, I was here.

4 – Which student is there?

5 – Whom do you want to see?

6 – Where do you want to go?

7 – When do you want to go?

8 – What train do you take?

9 – Some students stay late.

10 – Which is cheaper?

11 – Which one is more expensive?

Fritz-Meyer Sannon, PhD.

Exercise Q

<u>Underline the interrogative pronouns</u>

1 – <u>Which</u> one goes to Brooklyn?

2 – <u>What</u> was the right way to say?

3 – <u>Whom</u> do you want to talk to?

4 – <u>Who</u> came to dinner last night?

5 – <u>Which</u> one do you like?

6 – <u>Which</u> shirt do you want?

7 – <u>Whom</u> did you see yesterday?

8 – <u>What</u> day is today?

9 – <u>What</u> was your question?

10 – <u>Who</u> are you?

11 – <u>What</u> is your name?

12 – <u>What</u> is the best way to go to New Jersey?

<u>Exercise R</u>

<u>Indicate the indefinite pronouns by putting a checkmark</u>

1 – Why don't you give them some?

2 – Don't go now.

3 – I love everybody.

4 – Somebody left his wallet in class.

5 – No one shows up today.

6 – Give me many things today.

7 – I want some salt on my steak.

8 – I see somebody in the backyard.

9 – I want some.

10 – Everybody wants to go to Yankee Stadium.

11 – Many soldiers died in Vietnam.

12 – Some men are too cowardly.

Exercise S

Underlie the indefinite pronouns

1 – She likes many children.

2 – Every student has the same opportunity.

3 – I see something on my bed.

4 – Everybody has the same chance.

5 – I don't need much.

6 – I saw nobody.

7 – I don't see anybody.

8 – Somebody came this morning.

9 – Somebody called me up this morning.

10 – Nothing is good.

11 – I need some.

Exercise T

Indicate the adjective by putting "a" and the pronoun by putting "p" above the word

1 – Each man wins a prize.

2 – My friend is poor.

3 – That car is blue.

4 – I like to buy some.

5 – I want it.

6 – The women buy a lot of clothes.

7 – Those books are new.

8 – Those are mine.

9 – What is her name?

10 – What time is it?

11 – Every time I go there he is absent.

12 – I want much milk in my coffee.

Fritz-Meyer Sannon, PhD.

New English Grammar for ESL Students

University of Los Andes
Merida, Venezuela

Fritz-Meyer Sannon, PhD.

Chapter 5

Verbs

Definition: A verb (from Latin verbum: Word) is a word expressing an action performed by a subject (person or animal); a verb expresses also a state experienced by a subject (person or animal). In most languages, the verb is the most important part of the sentence.

Classification of Verbs

There are different kinds of verbs:

A – **Auxiliary verbs:** Are verbs that help other verbs to form some of their parts. They call them helping verbs, linking verbs.

Example: I have spoken; we shall go; you may leave; etc.

Fritz-Meyer Sannon, PhD.

B – **Action verbs:** Are verbs expressing actions; actions could be physical or mental.

Example: She <u>received</u> the ball. He <u>thinks</u> too much.

C – **Non action verbs:** Are verbs that do not express action performed by the subject.

Example: They look strong; he smells rat.

D – **Transitive verbs:** Are verbs requiring direct objects to complete the meaning of the sentence.

Example: Maria <u>cut</u> the roses. "Roses", is the direct object.

E – **Intransitive verbs:** Are verbs expressing actions without connection with the objects.

Example: My sister falls down.

F – **Regular verbs:** Are verbs that form the past tense by adding **"ed"**.

Example: finish, finished; talk, talked.

G – Irregular verbs: Are verbs that have the past completely different from the present.

Example: speak, spoke; see, saw; do, did, etc.

A – Auxiliary verbs: We call them "helping verbs," "aux," "modal auxiliaries".

The verb **"to be"** and the verb **"to have"** could be either auxiliaries or main verbs.

Here are the present, the past and the future of **"to be"**.

Present	Past	Future
I am	I was	I will be
You are	You were	You will be
He, she, it is	He, she, it was	He, she, it will be
We are	We were	We will be
You are	You were	You will be
They are	They were	They will be

Examples of **"to be"** as main verbs:

Fritz-Meyer Sannon, PhD.

*She **is** a doctor.*

*Sonia **was** in the library*

*We **are** strong.*

In those examples **"is"** and **"was"**, are not auxiliary verbs.

He **is** leaving; we **were** going to school; they **are** eating; **"is"**, **"were"**, and **"are"**, are auxiliary verbs.

Here are the present, past and future of **"to have"**.

Present	**Past**	**Future**
I have	I had	I will have
You have	You had	You will have
He, she, it has	He, she, it had	He, she, it will have
We have	We had	We will have
You have	You had	You will have
They have	They had	They will have

Some example of to have as main verbs.

Patricia **has** a beautiful car. In this example "**has**" is a main verb. "**Has**" means possess or own.

Carlos and Eduardo **had** a big house. "**Had**" is the main verb.

However in the following examples:

a) John "**has**" bought a motorcycle.

b) Denise "**has**" gone there.

c) Professor Fritz "**has**" seen that boy before.

d) She "**had**" sold her apartment.

In a) "**has**" is an auxiliary verb because it helps the verb bought.

In b) "**has**" is an auxiliary verb because it helps the verb gone.

In c) "**has**" is an auxiliary verb because it helps the verb seen.

In d) **"has"** is an auxiliary verb because it helps the verb sold.

There are also other auxiliary verbs such as:

<u>Do</u>, can, may, shall, will, would, ought to, must, should, could, might, etc.

Except "do" that becomes does in the third person singular, the other auxiliary verbs, or helping verbs or modals do not change in singular and plural; in affirmative, interrogative, negative forms.

I can swim.	I will visit.
You can swim.	You will visit.
He, she, can swim.	He, she, will visit.
We can swim.	We will swim.
You can swim.	You will visit.
They can swim.	They will visit.
Can I swim?	Will you visit?

Can she swim?   Will she visit?

However, with the auxiliary **"do"** it is different?

For instance:

I do know   I do remember

You do know   You do remember

He does know *   She does remember

etc.   etc.

Do you know?   Do we remember?

Do we know?   Do they remember?

Does she know?   Does she remember?

* Note that **he does know** is a *periphrastic form* meaning that instead of using inflection of the verb (he knows) we use the auxiliary verb **"do"** along with the main verb.

There are other *periphrastic modals* which have the same function like the modals, they help other verbs; they are also helping verbs.

Fritz-Meyer Sannon, PhD.

Here are some examples:

I can do it today.	I am able to do it today.
I will buy a car.	I am going to buy a car.
I must write a letter.	I have to write a letter.
I should give him the memo.	I ought to give him the memo.

New English Grammar for ESL Students

Exercises

Exercise A

Indicate by putting (aux) if the verb is an auxiliary verb or by putting (ma) if the verb is a main verb

1 – We have a good house.

2 – We are leaving the town.

3 – I have chosen another car.

4 – You are very bright.

5 – She has seen the same man.

6 – She is a very good student.

7 – My brother is leaving for California.

8 – Lionel had a Peugeot last year.

9 – The teacher was sick last Friday.

10 – We are giving away all we have.

11 – Rolanda and Irene will buy a piece of land in New Jersey.

Fritz-Meyer Sannon, PhD.

Exercise B

<ins>Underline the auxiliary verb where necessary</ins>

1 – My sister loves Antonio Aguilar.

2 – Her uncle <ins>is</ins> looking for you.

3 – The director is sick.

4 – My students are very motivated.

5 – I was absent from class yesterday.

6 – Mr. Williams had three small dogs.

7 – You are in the same classroom.

8 – My brother-in-law is not home.

9 – She was too nervous.

10 – We <ins>had</ins> bought a condo in the Dominican Republic.

11 – The teacher <ins>has</ins> visited the Metropolitan Museum of Art.

12 – My school is new.

13 – She <ins>is</ins> waving to her fiancé

14 – We have seen Miguel Aceves Mejia.

15 – We were working for President Balaguer.

Exercise C

<u>Underline all the modals in the following sentences</u>

1 – We shall overcome.

2 – What can I do for you?

3 – You should brush you teeth after each meal.

4 – My son can do it by himself.

5 – I will be there soon.

6 – May I leave the room.

7 – Would you do me a favor?

8 – Some students look very bright.

9 – May I help you?

10 – I couldn't believe what I saw.

11 – You should be there on time.

12 – She must be crazy.

Exercise D

In the following sentences underline all the periphrastic modals

1 – She <u>is not able to</u> carry the big suitcase.

2 – Maria may go home.

3 – She <u>was going to</u> take the cab when I called.

4 – "*El Diario La Prensa*" is a good newspaper.

5 – We <u>are going to</u> visit La Paz.

6 – She <u>is not allowed to</u> smoke in class.

7 – She <u>ought to</u> take Bayer aspirin in the morning.

8 – We went to Honduras last year.

9 – She <u>is allowed to</u> marry the African man.

10 – The New York Times <u>has to</u> make the correction.

11 – Bogota is a very beautiful city.

12 – If you don't leave now, you <u>will have to</u> pay more.

B – Action verbs: Action verbs express action. Action verbs could be transitive or intransitive. Actions can be physical or mental.

Here are some action verbs: **Eat, take, go, buy, think, speak, etc.**

Ex. John eats French fries. ("**Eat**" is a physical action verb; it is also a transitive verb)

Jean takes the book from the shelf. ("**Takes**" is a physical action verb; it is also a transitive verb.)

We go to Atlantic City. (**Go** is a physical action verb; but it is an intransitive verb.)

The girls buy candy at the store. ("**Buy**" is a physical action verb; it is also a transitive verb.)

Most of the students in my class speak Spanish. ("**Speak**" is a physical action verb; it is also a transitive verb.)

Note that the verb **"to speak"** although it is an action verb, it could be transitive or intransitive. (see section D and E)

Henri speaks too fast. (action and intransitive)

C – Non action verbs: Are verbs that do not express action performed by the subjects. Most of the verbs, linking verbs, or copulative verbs are usually followed by adjectives and not by adverbs.

Here are some non-action verbs:

<u>Be</u>: The boys are big. (Are links the adj. big to the subject boys)

<u>Appear</u>: She appears elegant.

<u>Become</u>: We become sick.

<u>Feel</u>: I feel happy.

<u>Look</u>: My fiancée looks clean.

<u>Smell</u>: That beautiful lady smells rat.

<u>Sound</u>: This sounds good.

Taste: The orange tastes very sweet.

Exercise A

Underline all action verbs in the following sentences if necessary

1 – She looks very tired this evening.

2 – She answers all the difficult questions.

3 – President Clinton went to Kosovo last month.

4 – May we go to the park?

5 – She loves me.

6 – Elizabeth bought a good bilingual dictionary.

7 – Give me two dollars and I will give you a ticket.

8 – There are more girls than boys in that school.

9 – How much are two and two?

10 – I don't know about that?

11 – He enjoyed going to school.

12 – She writes a letter to her mother every week.

Fritz-Meyer Sannon, PhD.

Exercise B

<u>Underline all action verbs and write at the end (action) where necessary</u>

1 – We get tired out.

2 – I smell the soup.

3 – We can touch the ceiling.

4 – I go to the park every Sunday.

5 – I sleep well at night.

6 – Could you please buy me a coffee?

7 – I watch television every morning.

8 – Stay there, I will bring it to you.

9 – My mother sends me a card.

10 – Did you see the plane?

11 – Everyday is a new day.

12 – She feels tired.

Exercise C

Put (a) after each action verb

1 – She bought (a) a bracelet for twenty dollars.

2 – Havana is the Capital of Cuba.

3 – We walk (a) in Central Park everyday.

4 – She will be in San Francisco.

5 – I don't love (a) that place; it is too quiet.

6 – Camaguey is a big city in Cuba.

7 – She knows (a) Port-au-Prince very well.

8 – There are twelve months in a year.

9 – She speaks (a) too fast.

10 – She speaks (a) Portuguese, Spanish and French.

Exercise D

Underline all the non-action or linking verbs

1 – We <u>get</u> really tired.

2 – She <u>looks</u> sick.

3 – She goes to Paris.

4 – We smell perfume in this class.

5 – That music sounds good.

6 – I smell the perfume.

7 – We saw Superman yesterday afternoon.

8 – That boy did not take a shower; he smells fish.

9 – She looks young.

10 – We bought plantains at the supermarket.

11 – We became crazy.

12 – The mangoes taste too sweet.

D – Transitive verbs: Are verbs requiring direct objects to complete the meaning of the sentence.

Example: Take, cut, give, buy, sell, etc.

a) *We took the book from the desk.* ("**Book**" is the direct object)

b) *The old man cut all the roses.* ("**Roses**" is the direct object)

c) *We give money to the church.* ("**Money**" is the direct object)

d) *My mother buys sugar from Associate.* ("**Sugar**" is the direct object)

e) *Conakry sold an old commercial airplane.* ("**Airplane**" is the direct object)

E - Intransitive verbs: Are verbs although expressing actions in most cases, have no direct objects; or the objects have no direct connection with the subject.

Example: Think, dream, go, insist, die.

a) *I think of her all the time.*

b) *She dreams about going to Acapulco.*

c) *We go to school by car.*

d) *You insist on the same mistake.*

Fritz-Meyer Sannon, PhD.

e) *The young footballer died a long time ago.*

Exercise A

Underline only the transitive verbs

1 – Puerto Rico exports raw materials to other countries.

2 – My daughter Fritzie will arrive tonight from Mexico.

3 – Bobby Capo was a very famous Puerto Rican singer.

4 – Believe it or not, the Big Apple has everything.

5 – Haiti is the largest island in the Caribbean Sea after Cuba.

6 – The "Lycée Pétion" has known many generations.

7 – Nancy has bought soda and milk for Hernando.

8 – My sister loves French fries.

9 – My mentor will understand that.

10 – Connie interviewed the congressman from California.

11 – I remember who built the Statue of Liberty.

12 – I won't accept any apology.

Exercise B

Underline each transitive verb in the following sentences

1 – The more you learn the more you earn.

2 – I don't believe in ghosts.

3 – Don't buy at the store.

4 – I believe you.

5 – I sold my car because I had problems.

6 – Take a chance and buy a lotto ticket.

7 – Today is my birthday.

8 – Since you are stupid, I will punish you.

9 – I tell you Montreal is cleaner than New York.

10 – I marry you because I love you.

11 – I saw a lot of rats in this train station.

12 – Don't laugh, my sister is pregnant again.

Exercise C

Write (t) above the transitive verbs and (I) above the intransitive verbs

1 – After the rain, the sun shines.

2 – Dolores went to Mexico last year.

3 – Monica dreamt that he won the jackpot.

4 – My wife bought a bedroom from "Westside" in Milford.

5 – Noemi has spoken to Jose.

6 – I think that walking is the best exercise.

7 – Silvia is one of the best students here.

8 – Nooria took the final test three times.

9 – The way to a man's heart is through his stomach.

10 – Kuesta looks very elegant.

11 – Saturday comes before Sunday.

12 – It takes two to tango.

F – Regular verbs: Are verbs (transitive or intransitive) that have their past tense and past participle in **"ed"**.

Call – called – called

Divide – divided – divided

Finish – finished – finished

Here are 100 most used regular verbs in alphabetical order.

Present	Past tense	Part participle or perfect
add	added	added
agree	agreed	agreed
apply	applied	applied
attend	attended	attended
believe	believed	believed
belong	belonged	belonged
benefit	benefited (use also benefitted)	benefited
celebrate	celebrated	celebrated
close	closed	closed

Fritz-Meyer Sannon, PhD.

connect	connected	connected
continue	continued	continued
decrease	decreased	decreased
declare	declared	declared
demand	demanded	demanded
determine	determined	determined
die	died	died
divide	divided	divided
dye	dyed	dyed
elect	elected	elected
eliminate	eliminated	eliminated
enclose	enclosed	enclosed
end	ended	ended
enjoy	enjoyed	enjoyed
establish	established	established
examine	examined	examined

exclude	excluded	excluded
expect	expected	expected
file	filed	filed
fill	filled	filled
finish	finished	finished
force	forced	forced
gain	gained	gained
hate	hated	hated
help	helped	helped
hope	hoped	hoped
improve	improved	improved
include	included	included
indicate	indicated	indicated
land	landed	landed
learn	learned	learned
lie	lied	lied

like	liked	liked
listen	listened	listened
live	lived	lived
look	looked	looked
love	loved	loved
mention	mentioned	mentioned
misinterpret	misinterpreted	misinterpreted
miss	missed	missed
mix	mixed	mixed
multiply	multiplied	multiplied
need	needed	needed
negotiate	negotiated	negotiated
note	noted	noted
notice	noticed	noticed
observe	observed	observed
open	opened	opened

owe	owed	owed
own	owned	owned
paint	painted	painted
participate	participated	participated
permit	permitted	permitted
pick	picked	picked
place	placed	placed
play	played	played
possess	possessed	possessed
present	presented	presented
prove	proved	proved
provide	provided	provided
push	pushed	pushed
receive	received	received
regard	regarded	regarded
represent	represented	represented

remain	remained	remained
report	reported	reported
reside	resided	resided
save	saved	saved
serve	served	served
smell	smelled	smelled
smile	smiled	smiled
smoke	smoked	smoked
start	started	started
state	stated	stated
stop	stopped	stopped
study	studied	studied
subtract	subtracted	subtracted
talk	talked	talked
touch	touched	touched
transfer	transferred	transferred

try	tried	tried
urge	urged	urged
use	used	used
visit	visited	visited
wait	waited	waited
want	wanted	wanted
warn	warned	warned
wave	waved	waved
walk	walked	walked
wash	washed	washed
work	worked	worked

G – Irregular verbs: The irregular verbs are those that have the past tense and the perfect completely different from the present tense. **Speak – spoke – spoken, take – took – taken, etc.**

Fritz-Meyer Sannon, PhD.

Few of them have the same form for the present, the past and the past participle.

cut – cut – cut; cost – cost – cost.

put – put – put; set – set – set.

Here are 100 most used irregular verbs listed in alphabetical order:

Present	Past tense	Part participle or perfect
arise	arose	arisen
awake	awoke	awaken
bear	bore	born
become	became	become
begin	began	begun
bind	bound	bound
bite	bit	bitten
blow	blew	blown
break	broke	broken

bring	brought	brought
build	built	built
buy	bought	bought
cast	cast	cast
choose	chose	chosen
come	came	come
cost	cost	cost
cut	cut	cut
deal	dealt	dealt
do	did	done
drink	drank	drunk
drive	drove	driven
eat	ate	eaten
fall	fell	fallen
feed	fed	fed
feel	felt	felt

Fritz-Meyer Sannon, PhD.

find	found	found
fly	flew	flown
forget	forgot	forgotten or forgot
forgive	forgave	forgiven
freeze	froze	frozen
get	got	gotten or got
give	gave	given
go	went	gone
grow	grew	grown
hear	heard	heard
hit	hit	hit
hold	held	held
keep	kept	kept
know	knew	known
lead	led	lead
leave	left	left

lend	lent	lent
let	let	let
lie	lay	laid
light	lit	lit
lose	lost	lost
mean	meant	meant
meet	met	met
pay	paid	paid
put	put	put
read	read	read
ride	rode	ridden
rise	rose	risen
run	ran	run
say	said	said
see	saw	seen
seek	sought	sought

Fritz-Meyer Sannon, PhD.

send	sent	sent
set	set	set
shake	shook	shaken
shine	shone	shone
shoot	shot	shot
show	showed	shown
shut	shut	shut
sing	sang	sung
sit	sat	sat
sleep	slept	slept
slit	slit	slit
speak	spoke	spoken
speed	sped	sped
spend	spent	spent
split	split	split
spread	spread	spread

spring	sprang	sprung
stand	stood	stood
steal	stole	stolen
stick	stuck	stuck
stink	stank	stunk
strike	struck	struck
swear	swore	swore
sweep	swept	swept
swim	swam	swum
take	took	taken
teach	taught	taught
tear	tore	torn
tell	told	told
think	thought	thought
throw	threw	thrown
understand	understood	understood

Fritz-Meyer Sannon, PhD.

upset	upset	upset
wake	woke	woke
wear	wore	wore
weave	wove	woven
wed	wed	wed
weep	wept	wept
wet	wet	wet
win	won	won
wind	wound	wound
write	wrote	written

Exercises

Exercise A

Change the following from present to past tense

1 – She understands very well the lesson today.

2 – They spend too much money in food.

3 – Mr. Fritz teaches English grammar.

4 – She never attends school in summer.

5 – She swears to tell the truth.

6 – The little girl sweeps the floor today.

7 – They drive from New York to Atlanta.

8 – Every time she drinks coffee, she throws up.

9 – The mother feeds her baby very well.

10 – We forget to decorate the green room.

11 – They know many English words.

12 – Claudia tells her mother she is going to get married.

13 – She sees everything.

14 – Those people travel all the time.

15 – This lesson seems very difficult.

16 – They go there every year.

Exercise B

Use the present or past tense where necessary in the space provided

1 – Arani (to live) (……………..) there last year.

2 – She (to leave) (……………..) years ago.

3 – Last year we (to go) (……………..) to Bangladesh.

4 – I (to give) (………………) you two dollars each day for breakfast.

5 – Charles (to be) (……………) in Chicago from 1998-2000.

6 – You and I (to go) (……………..) to the football game.

7 – Yesterday (to be) (……………) Monday. Today (to be) (………..) Tuesday.

8 – We (understand) (……………..) him very well when he talked.

9 – If you (to love) (………………) me, I (to love) (………………..) you too.

10 – She (to put) (…………………) the plate on the table.

11 – We (to misunderstand) (…………… you, when you (to testify) (……………) last week.

12 – I (to go) (……….) to school; yesterday I (to be) (…………) late.

13 – My mother (to die) (………………) a long time ago.

14 – My friend is sick, he (to be) (…………..) in the hospital.

15 – She was drunk and she (to cut) (……………) herself.

16 – I (to be) (……………) in good health now, last year I (to be) (…………..) sick.

17 – I (to live) (……………) on Broadway now.

Fritz-Meyer Sannon, PhD.

Auxiliary verbs interrogative and negative form

We make questions with auxiliary verbs by placing the verbs before the subject.

Examples: Are you sick? Were you sick? Can you talk?

Affirmative form of auxiliary verbs or modals

I am	I have	I can
you are	you have	you can
he, she is	he, she has	he, she can
we are	we have	we can
you are	you have	you can
they are	they have	they can
I was	I had	I could
you were	you had	you could
he, she was	he, she had	he, she could
we were	we had	we could
you were	you had	you could

they were   they had   they could

Interrogative form of auxiliary verbs

am I?   * have I?   can I?

are you?   have you?   can you?

is he, she?   has he, she?   can he, she?

are we?   have we?   can we?

are you?   have you?   can you?

are they?   have they?   can they?

* Note that **"to have"** could be an auxiliary verb or could be an irregular main verb. *Example: I <u>have</u> gone, he <u>has</u> spoken*

"Have" and **"has"** are auxiliary or helping verbs. The question form is: Have I gone?

Has he spoken?

Fritz-Meyer Sannon, PhD.

However **"to have"** is an irregular verb in the following example:

My father <u>has</u> two buildings.

"Has" is the main verb, it is an irregular verb. The question form is: Does my father have two buildings?

(See next chapter)

Negative form of auxiliary verbs

We form the negative by placing "not" after the verb.

Examples:

Affirmative

I am	I have	I can
You are	You have	You can
She is	He has	He can
etc.	etc.	etc.
I was	I have	I could
You were	You have	You could

He was	She was	He could
etc.	etc.	etc.

Negative

I am not	I have not	I can not
You are not	You have not	You can not
She is not	He has not	He can not
etc.	etc.	etc.

I was not	I have not	I could not
You were not	You have not	You could not
He was not	She was not	He could not
etc.	etc.	etc.

Interrogative form or question form

Every time we make questions in English we use the auxiliary **"do"** at the beginning of the question for all persons except in the third person singular we use **"does."**

Examples:

Fritz-Meyer Sannon, PhD.

You take it seriously?

Do you take it seriously?

The students have the class.

Do the students have the class?

We buy the same clothes.

Do we buy the same clothes?

The teacher likes me.

Does the teacher like me?

She loves flowers.

Does she love flowers?

What about the negative form?

We form the negative by placing **"do not"** or **"does not"** before the main verb.

Examples: We go to the movie.

We do not go to the movie.

The men know it well.

The men do not know it well.

My parents live far away.

My parents do not live far away.

My sister drives.

My sister does not drive.

My sister learns Spanish.

My sister does not learn Spanish.

Interrogative or question form in past tense

To make questions in the past tense we use the auxiliary **"did"** at the beginning of the sentence.

Examples: The man went to the football game.

Did the man go to the football game?

The woman bought flowers.

Did the woman buy the flowers?

As you have noticed by using "did" you have to change the main verb to the infinitive form. However, with auxiliary verbs, with modals you do not have to use do or did when you make questions.

We were very happy yesterday.

Question form: Were we very happy yesterday?

We will go to Cancun next year.

Question form: Will we go to Cancun next year?

Mercedes may buy a new house.

Question form: May Mercedes buy a new house?

Exercises

Exercise A

Change to question form

1 – She went to Brooklyn on Labor Day.

2 – Victor Hugo wrote "Les Misérables."

3 – My grandparents came from China.

4 – My friend was in the hospital.

5 – She lived in Brooklyn.

6 – She left the Airport very late last night.

7 – She made a very good impression.

8 – They bought a piece of land.

9 – They fought very hard.

10 – She was very quiet.

11 – Many students stayed home yesterday.

12 – She looked like her sister.

Exercise B

Change to Question, (interrogative) form

1 – My teacher will go to Guatemala next year.

2 – Your name is Rodrigo.

3 – She went to Yankee Stadium last night.

4 – Adriana and Ramon studied together.

5 – My girlfriend will go to Cojutepeque.

6 – My mother gave me a cake.

7 – She is leaving now for Tunisia.

8 – She cuts the meat with an old knife.

9 – My brother goes to the Immigration office today.

10 – You like the USA very much.

11 – She put the book on the teacher's desk yesterday.

12 – Africa is a very rich continent.

Negative form in the past

To change to negative form in the past we put **"did not"** before the main verb.

She went to church.

Negative form: She did not go to church.

Mary and Fritz bought fruits at Bravo.

Negative form: Mary and Fritz did not buy fruits at "Bravo."

He tried to enter the room without authorization.

Negative form: He did not try to enter the room without authorization.

As you have noticed, by putting **"did not"** before the main verb, we change the sentence to negative form. However, with auxiliary verbs or helping verbs you just put **"not'** after the auxiliary verbs for the negative form.

Fritz-Meyer Sannon, PhD.

We were very happy.

Negative: We were not very happy.

We might go to Cancun.

Negative: We might not go to Cancun.

Mercedes could buy that house.

Negative: Mercedes could not buy that house.

Exercise A

<u>Change to negative form</u>

1 – Students and teachers went to the library.

2 – She gave me candies from Santo Domingo.

3 – My brother bought a beautiful shirt at Macy's.

4 – ESL students at Queens EOC are good people.

5 – The shoemakers went on strike.

6 – She wrote to her mother many times.

7 – The man knew the names of all the students.

8 – The prisoners were hungry and angry.

9 – The girl over there looked very strange.

10 – Dad gave fifty dollars to Ricky.

11 – The sharks attacked the young men.

Exercise B

Change to negative form

1 – She was late yesterday.

2 – Yesterday was Monday.

3 – She had "Bandera paisa" last night.

4 – The Palestinians killed about 100 Israelis.

5 – The Chinese workers live in the same neighborhood.

6 – She spent the whole year in Chicago.

7 – We were in Peru.

8 – We had to finish the work.

9 – We were permitted to smoke in the lobby.

10 – She has bought an old Chevrolet.

11 – She might spend the weekend in Greenwich, Connecticut.

Question words commonly used

When: **When** are you leaving for California?

Where: **Where** are you going to school?

Why: **Why** do you buy it?

How: **How** old are you?

How cold: **How cold** is it?

How far: **How far** do you go?

How fast: **How fast** does she go?

How long: **How long** have you been here?

How much: **How much** is it?

How soon: **How soon** is he coming?

Whose: **Whose** car is that?

What: **What** is your first name?

What about: **What about** the last lesson?

What kind: **What kind of perfume?**

Which: **Which one is better?**

Fritz-Meyer Sannon, PhD.

New English Grammar for ESL Students

Legendary Citadel
One of the wonders of the world.
Haiti

Fritz-Meyer Sannon, PhD.

Chapter 6

Periphrastic Modals and Linking Verbs

A – We have already studied in chapter 5 the modals and their function in the sentences.

Let's talk again about the modals and their equivalents: the periphrastic modals along with the linking verbs…

The most common modals and the corresponding periphrastic modals are:

Can ————————————-To be able to

May ————————————-To be allowed to

Shall/will ———————————-To be going to

Must ————————————To have to

Should ————————————-Ought to (to be supposed to, would better)

Foreign students have a tendency of generalizing by adding "s" in the 3rd person singular.

He cans do that. (incorrect)

He can do that. (correct)

They tend also to add "to" after the modals.

He must to go. (incorrect)

He must go. (correct)

He may to leave soon. (incorrect)

He may leave soon. (correct)

He could to take the book. (incorrect)

He could take the book. (correct)

Modals (from Latin modus) express some attitude toward a state or an action as a wish, a possibility or advice. They are also called *modal-auxiliaries*. The modal auxiliary is rarely used alone, always with the main verb in the sentence.

Examples:

a) We <u>should brush</u> our teeth after each meal.

b) We <u>must stop</u> at the red light.

c) I <u>may be</u> there before noon.

d) She <u>might go</u> to Guayaquil.

e) I <u>will leave</u> for Bogota.

As we have seen the modals are helping verbs.

Modals cannot function by themselves; they are followers meaning they help other verbs; they cannot express the main ideas. *Examples:*

1 – He may to Chicago (incorrect)

2 – We will soon (incorrect)

3 – We must today (incorrect)

4 – Mary might tomorrow (incorrect)

The above sentences (1, 2, 3, 4,) do not make sense by themselves; they cannot express the main ideas.

As we said before, all of the modals have their counterparts.

For instance:

Can ——————————————-To be able to

The past time or conditional form is "could" what about the future time?

I will can. (incorrect)

I will be able to. (correct)

Must ——————————————-To have to

What is the past tense of must?

What is the future tense of must?

I will must (incorrect) we cannot use two modals together)

I will have to see (future) (correct)

I had to see (past) (correct)

May ——————————————To be permissible, to be allowed

In fact, the past tense is **"might"** the conditional has the same form **"might."**

What about the future?

John may use the room today.

John will may the room tomorrow. (incorrect)

John will be allowed to use the room tomorrow. (correct)

What about "shall" or "will"? "Shall" is rarely used in USA except in formal situations. **"Will"** is used in American English. However both **"shall"** and **"will"** express the future action. What about expressing some action in the past with **"intention"** in the future?

Will ———————————————- To be going to

Examples: Today I will cook for Dad.

Yesterday I was going to cook for Dad.

Fritz-Meyer Sannon, PhD.

Linking Verbs

Some grammarians define linking verbs as auxiliary verbs or copulas that serve to link subjects and predicates (action or state expressed by the subject).

Examples: John smells good (linking verb)
or
The baby tastes sweet (linking verb)

In those two sentences **"smells"** or **"tastes"** have one interpretation, they are linking verbs and can be replaced only by the verb "to be."

But if we say:

a) John smells rat.

or

b) The baby tastes vinegar.

Smells could be a **"linking"** verb or an **"action"** verb. Therefore, the same verb could have two interpretations.

c) <u>John smells rat</u>.

John does not do any action. **"Smells"** is a linking verb. A third person does the action.

"Smells" is an action verb. *Example: John smells the rat.* Here, John does the action of smelling the rat. **"Rat"** is the direct object of smells.

d) <u>The baby tastes vinegar</u>.

Here, the baby does not do any action. His mother does the action of tasting the baby.

"Tastes" is an action verb. *Example: The baby tastes the vinegar.* In this case, the baby does the action of tasting the vinegar and vinegar is the direct object of **"tastes."**

In short, linking verbs are those followed by a word group that describes the subject.

They are:

1) <u>Appear</u>: The little boy <u>appears</u> nervous.

2) <u>Become</u>: She <u>becomes</u> sick.

3) <u>Feel</u>: Mary <u>feels</u> very sad.

4) <u>Grow</u>: The tree <u>grows</u> tall.

5) <u>Look</u>: My fiancée <u>looks</u> beautiful.

6) <u>Remain</u>: They <u>remain</u> calm.

7) <u>Seem</u>: Martha <u>seems</u> very happy.

8) <u>Smell</u>: The old man <u>smells</u> bad.

9) <u>Sound</u>: It <u>sounds</u> great to me.

10) <u>Taste</u>: The coffee <u>tastes</u> too sweet.

Remember linking verbs are usually followed by adjectives not by adverbs; all the above linking verbs can be replaced by the verb to be ("**is**", "**are**", "**was**", "**were**", "**will be**", **etc.**)

New English Grammar for ESL Students

Exercises

Exercise A

Write (C) after the correct sentences and (INC) after the incorrect ones.

1 – She cans go home.

2 – Could you do that?

3 – I shall be going to Yankee Stadium.

4 – I am allowed to talk in class.

5 – I cannot do nothing.

6 – Today is a beautiful day.

7 – The rat can eat the mouse.

8 – I will be there before 5 o'clock.

9 – She will must visit her doctor.

Exercise B

Fill in the blank with a modal or a periphrastic modal if possible. Write "NA" if it is not possible.

1 – I … going to California in December.

2 – You … to do it when we want.

3 – We … not take our vacation now.

4 – Teresa … very smart now.

5 – You … stop at the red light.

6 - …   you tell what time it is.

7 – My sister is … to see a doctor soon.

8 – You … avoid smoking.

9 – She … go to California in July.

10 – You … to smoke in class.

Exercise C

Underline the linking verbs

1 – They are from Cap-Haïtien.

2 – She smells good.

3 – We were in Puerto Rico.

4 – Alexandria looks very clean.

5 – Silvia bought a brand new car.

6 – She appears in good health.

7 – This music sounds great.

8 – She took a long vacation.

9 – The drink tastes very good.

Exercise D

Underline the modals

1 – Soldiers <u>should</u> be real heroes.

2 – You <u>may</u> not smoke here.

3 – <u>Can</u> you go to the stadium.

4 – We <u>should</u> study seriously.

5 – My cousin was ill.

6 – They <u>may</u> go tomorrow.

7 – We <u>shall</u> overcome.

8 – I <u>must</u> be there.

9 – <u>May</u> I help you?

10 – She went to Washington by herself.

Exercise E

<u>Change the adjectives following the linking verbs by another adjective.</u>

1 – My friend smells rat.

2 – The little boy tastes salt.

3 – My boss sounds upset.

4 – Marina is very beautiful.

5 – Jean looks very tired.

6 – Yvonne was tired.

7 – Joseph becomes sick.

8 – The child smells good.

9 – The food tastes bad.

Exercise F

Change the following modals to periphrastic modals by keeping the same meaning

1 – The students must go to the library.

2 – Professor Fritz can play ping-pong.

3 – My teacher may go to California soon.

4 – They should stop doing it.

5 – We may go to Bankha next year.

6 – All people here must leave the room.

7 – We shall go soon.

8 – The lady cannot stay here.

9 – My wife will not buy this house.

10 – My son should wash his hands.

Fritz-Meyer Sannon, PhD.

Types of houses in the old Port-Au-Prince
Haiti

Fritz-Meyer Sannon, PhD.

Chapter 7

Mood/Tenses of Verbs

Definition: Mood (from French mode; from Latin: modus, manner, measure, form) refers to the verb form indicating whether what is said or written is certain, possible, necessary, doubtful or desirable.

There are different kinds of mood:

A – Infinitive

B – Participle

C – Indicative

D – Conditional

E – Imperative

F – Subjunctive

Fritz-Meyer Sannon, PhD.

A. <u>Infinitive Mood</u> (Form Latin: Infinitivus) is the form of the verb usually with "to" (not always).

Example: I don't have anything to <u>say</u>.

<u>To be</u> or not <u>to be</u>.

There are two forms of infinitives:

Active voice – Present Infinitive: <u>to buy</u>

Perfect Infinitive: <u>to have bought</u>

Passive voice – Present Infinitive: <u>to be bought</u>

Perfect Infinitive: <u>to have been bought</u>.

Examples:

<u>Present Infinitive:</u>

a) Active voice – I want to go to school.

Would you like to eat with me?

Alma wants to buy a Mercedes.

b) Passive voice – She doesn't want to be invited.

We do not want to be seen.

She doesn't expect to be welcome.

B. Participle (From Latin: participium = sharing) is an adjective form of the verb, ending in "ing" (present participle) or "ed," "en," etc (past participle). Participles are used in verb phrases. (I am giving her some money or I have given her some money) or as adjectives (embarrassing situation).

There are two forms of participles:

a) **Active voice** – Present participle: giving

Past participle: given

b) **Passive voice** – Present participle: being given

Past participle: been given

C. **Indicative Mood** is the form of the verb stating a fact, the truth.

Ex. The earth is round. I saw the doctor. I have been there, etc.

Indicative mood has different tenses or forms taken by the verb to show the time of the action or occurrence whether in the present, in the past, or future or continuing or completed.

Here are the tenses:

Present tense

a) Active voice -

I give

You give

She, he gives

We give

You give

note: We use the present tense to express an habitual action, a general statement of fact.

Examples: I go to school by bus every day. The earth is round, etc.

They give

b) Passive voice -

I am given

You are given

She, he is given

We are given

You are given

They are given

Past tense

a) Active voice -

I gave

You gave

She, he gave

We gave

You gave

They gave

note: We use the past tense when we describe an action which took place at some definite time in the past.

Examples: I saw the boy yesterday. I bought a house last year.

b) Passive voice -

I was given

You were given

She, he was given

We were given

You were given

They were given

Simple future tense

a) Active voice -

I will give

You will give

She, he will give

We will give

You will give

They will give

note: We use the future tense when we express an action that will happen in the future. We use will for determination or to be going to (intention). Both are correct. Shall is not Usually used in USA.

b) Passive voice –

I will be given

You will be given

She, he will be given

We will be given

You will be given

They will be given

Present perfect

a) Active voice -

I have given

You have   given

She, he has given

We have given

You have given

They have given

note: We use the present perfect in two situations

a) When we describe an action which took place at some indefinite time in the past.

Example: I have seen that movie.

b) When we describe an

b) Passive voice -

I have been given

You have been given

She, he has been given

We have been given

You have been given

They have been given

action which began in the past and continues up to the present.

Example: I have been in New York for two years or I have been in New York since 2001.

Present continuous (progressive)

a) Active voice -

I am giving

You are giving

She, he is giving

We are giving

You are giving

They are giving

<u>note</u>: we use the present continuous when we describe an action which takes place now, at the present moment.

Example: Fritz is talking to Xiomara.

b) Passive voice –

I am being given

You are being given

She, he is being given

We are being given

You are being given

They are being given

Past perfect

a) Active voice -

I had given

You had given

She, he had given

We had given

You had given

They had given

note: We use the past perfect to express an action that was completed before another occurred.

Example: I had finished when she came.

Fritz-Meyer Sannon, PhD.

Passive voice –

b) I had been given

You had been given

She, he had been given

We had been given

You had been given

They had been given

Past continuous (progressive)

a) Active voice -

I was giving

You were giving

She, he was giving

We were giving

You were giving

They were giving

<u>note</u>: We use the past continuous when we express an action in progress in the past. Ex. I was speaking. Or when two actions are in progress in the past. *Example: While I was*

cooking, my husband was talking on the phone.

Passive voice -

b) I was being given

You were being given

She, he was being given

We were being given

You were being given

They were being given

Future perfect

a) Active voice -

I will have given

You will have given

She, he will have given

We will have given

note: We use the future perfect when we express an action that will be completed before an other action in the future.

Example: I will have

You will have given *terminated when you*

They will have given *come.*

Passive voice (rare) -

b) I will have been given

You will have been given

She, he will have been given

We will have been given

You will have been given

They will have been given

Present perfect continuous

a) Active voice -

I have been giving

You have been giving

She, he has been giving

We have been giving

You have been giving

<u>note</u>: We use the present perfect continuous when we describe an action which began in the past and continuous up to the present.

Example: I have been living

They have been giving   *here for 2 years.*

Passive voice –

b) **Unused in Modern American English**

Past perfect continuous

a) **Active voice:**

I had been giving

You had been giving

She, he had been giving

We had been giving

You had been giving

They had been giving

Passive voice –

b) **Unused in Modern American English**

Future perfect continuous

a) Active voice -

I will have been giving

You will have been giving

She, he will have been giving

We will have been giving

You will have been giving

They will have been giving

Passive voice –

b) Unused in Modern American English

note: We use the future perfect continuous to express an action in the future which is in progress before another action in the future.

D. Conditional Mood (from Latin: Conditio = agreement, condition) is the form of the verb that expresses a condition or supposition; a from that contains, implies a condition.

Examples: She would go there. She would have gone there.

a) **Active voice** – Present conditional: would give

Past conditional: would have given

b) **Passive voice:** Present conditional: would be given

Past conditional: would have be given

Examples:

a) *If I won the Lotto, I would give one million dollars for charity.*

b) *If I had won the Lotto, I would have given one million dollars to charity.*

c) *If she were nice, she would be given a lot of money.*

d) *If she had come earlier, she would have be given a lot of money.*

E. <u>Imperative mood</u> (from Latin: Imperativus, imperare = to command) is a form of the verb that expresses

exhortation or command. In an imperative sentence, the subject is really "you", but it is always understood.

Example: "close the door"... is (you) close the door.

In modern American English only one form (one tense) of imperative mood is used: Present imperative in the active or passive voice.

a) Active voice –

Present: give

Past: no

Future: none

b) Passive voice –

Present: be given

Past: none (unused)

Future: none (unused)

Example: Give and you will receive

Be given (rare)

F. Subjunctive mood (from Latin: subjunctivus, subjungere = to subjoin, to add, to append) Subjunctive is the form of the verb that denotes an act which is not a "fact", something that is desirable, possible or conditional; a form that expresses uncertainties or wishes.

Example: If I were a millionaire, I would build a modern school for Queens EOC.

Present tense

a) **Active voice** –

If I give

If you give

If she, he give

If we give

If you give

If they give

Passive voice –

b) If I be given

If you be given

If she, he be given

If we be given

If you be given

If they be given

Past tense

a) Active voice –

If I gave

If you gave

If she, he gave

If we gave

If you gave

If they gave

Passive voice –

b) If I were given

If you were given

If she, he were given

If we were given

If you were given

If they were given

Future tense

a) Active voice –

If I should give

If you should give

If she, he should give

If we should give

If you should give

If they should give

Fritz-Meyer Sannon, PhD.

Passive voice –

b) If I should be given

If you should be given

If she, he should be given

If we should be given

If you should be given

If they should be given

G. Sequence of tenses

"Sequence of tenses" means that the tense of the verb in the subordinate clause depends on the tense of the verb in the main clause.

For example:

a) **If I have money, I will buy a house**

b) **If I had money, I would buy a house.**

c) **If I had money, I would have bought a house.**

1 – Let's review: **sequence of tenses** with infinitives:

We use the infinitive form (with to: **to go, to speak, to swim,** etc.) to show that the action expresses by the infinitive occurs after the action expressed in the main clause.

Example: I hope to go in Puerto Rico. (The action of **"to go"** in Puerto Rico occurs after **"I hope"**) He has hoped to give her all his money. (The action of **"to give"** occurred later than the action of to hope.)

However, we use the perfect infinitive form (to have followed) by the past participle for action which took place earlier than the action expressed by the main verb in the sentence.

Example:

I would like to have gone to the baseball game. The action of **"to have gone"** occurred earlier than the action of **"would like"**.

Another example:

I regret not "to have bought' the car. **"To have bought"** is a perfect infinitive. Note that the action of **"to have bought"** occurred long time before the action of **"regret"**.

2 – <u>Sequence of tenses with participles</u>

As we have already studied, there are two forms of participle: Present Participle (**ing** form, speaking, going) Past Participle (ed form, washed, spoken) Like the infinitive, we use the present participle **(ing)** when the action occurs at the same time as the action expressed by the main verb of the sentence.

Examples:

"Looking" at the window, I feel very happy. She is so glad "taking" a nap. As we have noted, the actions of **"looking"** and **"taking"** occur at the same time as **"feel"** and **"be glad."**

We use the **"past participle"** (**spoken, given, taken,** etc.) or perfect participle (**having spoken, having given, having taken,** etc.) when the action expressed by the past participle occurred earlier than the action of the main verb of the sentence.

Examples:

Once the plane taken off, she left the airport. **"Taken off"** took place earlier than **"she left."** *After having giving her the passport, they ran away.* The action of *"**having given**"* took place before the action of running away.

3 – Sequence of tenses with Indicative future

When the verb in the **"if"** clause is in the present tense, we use the present or the future in the main clause.

Examples:

If you come today, I will give you your book.

If I have money, I will buy a car

Fritz-Meyer Sannon, PhD.

Or

If you come today, I give you your book.

If I have money, I buy a car.

Note: it is permissible to use both forms.

However, when the verb in the **"if"** clause is in the past, it is important to use the present conditional form. (**would + verb**)

Examples:

If you came, I would take you to the park.

If I won the Lotto, I would buy a house.

When the verb in the **"if"** clause is in the past perfect tense, the verb in the main clause is in the past conditional.

Examples: If I had come, you would have left it for me.

If you had been here, we would have given you something.

Note that there are two different situations: real situation or unreal (contrary to the fact) situation.

If I was there, my team would win the game. (This is a real situation; it is possible that I be there. It is a fact that I could be there. That is a real situation.)

However if we say:

If I were Charles, I would not marry Camilla. This is not possible I be the Prince Charles. That is an unreal situation; a situation that is contrary to the fact.

There is also another unreal situation: If I had won the Lotto in Germany, I would have bought two big buildings in Manhattan. First, I never gamble; second, I did not play. Third, I don't even know where Germany is located. Again this is another unreal situation, contrary to the fact.

Exercises

Exercise A

Use the present tense of the verbs in parenthesis; then, change from present to past tense

1 – The workers……………(live) in California.

2 – The nurse……………..(come) from California.

3 – I will buy a house, if I……………(have) money.

4 – She………………..(work) in California and he……………(live) in New York.

5 – My grandmother…………………..(speak) English to them.

6 – Esther…………………(to be) very beautiful.

7 – My mother………………(sleep) too much.

8 – The students……………..(become) very lazy.

9 – My friend and I………………..(look) very happy today.

10 – She………………..(go) to the movies by herself.

Exercise B

Change the verbs from present tense to present progressive (or present continuous)

1 – I eat well.

2 – The boys play soccer well.

3 – My mother cooks chicken.

4 – The old man walks with a heavy cane.

5 – My co-workers collect for the sick supervisor.

6 – My father goes to the movie.

7 – My classmates talk to the principal.

8 – My friend studies in the living room.

9 – The girls play volleyball in the backyard.

Exercise C

Change the verbs from present tense to present perfect

1 – Boys come in the morning.

Fritz-Meyer Sannon, PhD.

2 – The deer eat everything in my backyard.

3 – The CNN journalist mentions US linguistic arrogance.

4 – Carline has a beautiful piano.

5 – My wife plays guitar.

6 – She speaks many languages.

7 – She want to move to Atlanta, Georgia.

8 – My friend Clause lives in Florida.

9 – The wild turkeys come early today.

10 – My father lives in Boca Raton.

11 – I buy a beautiful condo in Darien, CT.

Exercise D

Change the verbs to past perfect tense 1 – She bought a brand new car.

2 – The teachers of Queens EOC are celebrating Khariyyah's birthday.

3 – The ESL III students learn very fast.

4 – My children were in Boca Chica.

5 – The men from the other team die in a plane accident.

6 – She put the car in the garage.

7 – My friend went to Chicago with her dad.

8 – She left the city long time ago.

Exercise E

<u>Change the following verbs to future perfect</u>

1 – John and Nora go to Nicaragua.

2 – My brothers receive a good package.

3 – Carmen plays volleyball very well.

4 – Isabel and Yolanda study together.

5 – My friend receives a scholarship.

6 – Juan and Jorge bring chalk to the teacher.

7 – Clara and Isabel go to Mexico together.

8 – Xiomara wins 10 million dollars today.

9 – Marina sells her house in New York.

10 – Julio works very hard.

Exercise F

Change the verb to future perfect continuous

1 – She buys a beautiful boat.

2 – They fight very hard in Brazil.

3 – My brothers go to Panama.

4 – They play in the park.

5 – My parents come home.

6 – The students go to California.

7 – Isabel buys a house in Cancun.

8 – She will take a big vacation.

Exercise G

Change to past continuous

1 – She buys a condo today.

2 – She runs all day.

3 – The soldiers leave the barracks.

4 – My friend eats too much.

5 – The boys run in the park.

6 – My children got to Toys R' Us.

7 – She plays cards with her sister.

8 – She has a brick house.

9 – I swim in the pool.

10 – My brothers get a vacation house.

11 – My professor plays tennis well.

Exercise H

Write "C" after the correct form of the verb and "INC" after the incorrect form

1 – She leave school everyday at 7:30 p.m.

2 – If you like me, I like you.

3 – My father went to Guatemala next week.

4 – She has been living for 25 years.

5 – Margarita is in Venezuela yesterday.

6 – If you cans stand the heat, get out of the kitchen.

7 – She puts her book on the desk.

8 – My daughter and I goes to church.

9 – My grandmother put her purse on the bed.

Exercise I

In the blank spaces, use the correct form of the verbs

1 – If I have money I……………….(buy) a house.

2 – I need a raincoat if it………………(rain).

3 – I would have taken the train if I………………….(have) money.

4 – My teacher is……………….(teach) now.

5 – She……………….(live) in New York since 1987.

6 – If Barbara Walters……………..(be) a man she……………(have) a lot of success.

7 – If she……………….(have) money she would buy a house.

8 – I wish she…………………(be) very rich.

9 – She……………….(cook) now.

10 – Maria………………..(play) dominoes at the same time yesterday.

11 – If I ……………….(be) a woman I would not wear pants.

Fritz-Meyer Sannon, PhD.

New English Grammar for ESL Students

Museum of Art
Ponce, Puerto Rico

Fritz-Meyer Sannon, PhD.

Chapter 8

Adverbs

Definition: An adverb (from Latin adverbium) is a word that modifies a verb, an adjective or another adverb. Do not confuse adverb and adjective. Adverbs modify verbs, adjectives and adverbs whereas adjectives describe or modify nouns or pronouns.

There are different types of adverbs:

A – Adverbs of degree

B – Adverbs of duration

C – Adverbs of emphasis

D – Adverbs of frequency

E – Adverbs of interrogation or interrogative adverbs.

F – Adverbs of manner

G – Mid-sentence adverbs

H – Adverbs of place

I – Adverbs of probabilities

J – Adverbs of time

K – Conjunctive adverbs

A – Adverbs of degree

The adverbs of degree tell us the degree or the extent of an event. They are:

1 – **Adequately:** Queens EOC is adequately equipped

2 – **Strongly:** We strongly agree with Mrs. Smith.

3 – **Totally:** She is totally correct.

4 – **Entirely:** I have entirely finished with the project.

5 – **Immensely:** She covers immensely the whole area.

B – Adverbs of duration

The adverbs of duration tell us how long some activities last. They are:

1 – **Briefly**

2 – **Indefinitely**

3 – **Permanently**

4 – **Temporarily**

5 – **Forever**

1 – Let's pay a visit briefly to our classmates.

2 – Don't worry, you can use it indefinitely.

3 – Believe me, you can stay here permanently.

4 – You can have this job temporarily.

5 – I love you forever.

C – Adverbs of emphasis

The adverbs of emphasis, as the name indicates, emphasize on the action performed by the verbs. They are:

1 – **Certainly**

2 – **Absolutely**

3 – **Positively**

4 – **Really**

5 – **Simply**

1 – We certainly love our school

2 – Nellie absolutely loves to go to Haiti.

3 – Regina positively wants to speak English well.

4 – He really likes to live in California.

5 – I simply tell you the way it is.

D – Adverbs of frequency

The adverbs of frequency or frequency adverbs are used to show how after things happen. They are placed before the main verbs. Adverbs of frequency usually come after the first auxiliary verbs if any.

The adverbs of frequency or frequency adverbs are:

1 – **Seldom**

2 – **Never**

3 – Sometimes

4 – Often

5 – Frequently

1 – She seldom participates in class.

2 – My father never goes to Atlantic City.

3 – She sometimes wakes up at 10 o'clock on weekends.

4 – Juan has often been absent from class.

5 – I frequently go to church.

E – Adverbs of interrogation or interrogative adverbs

Adverbs of interrogation or interrogative adverbs are usually placed at the beginning of the sentences and are used to ask questions. They are never placed in the middle of the sentence or at the end. They are:

1 – **How**

2 – **When**

3 – **Why**

4 – Where

1 – How do you fix it?

2 – When will you go there?

3 – Why will Donna sing in that church?

4 – Where did he put my coat?

F – Adverbs of manner

The adverbs of manner tell us how the things are done. Sometimes, we add **"-ly"** to the adjectives to form the adverbs. *Examples:*

1 – Bad – **Badly**

2 – Elegant – **Elegantly**

3 – Nice – **Nicely**

4 – Quick – **Quickly**

5 – Weak – **Weakly**

1 – Pedro is a bad driver; he drives so badly.

2 – She walks elegantly.

3 – Margarita knows how to wait on customers; she does it so nicely.

4 – She finished the job quickly.

5 – That old man is sick, he walks weakly.

If the adjectives end in **"y"**, the **"y"** changes to **"i"** before **"-ly"** is added.

Examples:

*1 – Busy – **Busily***

*2 – Happy – **Happily***

*3 – Easy – **Easily***

*4 – Crazy – **Crazily***

*5 – Angry – **Angrily***

1 – They work busily.

2 – They all welcome me happily.

3 – The students finish their homework easily.

4 – In this office workers act crazily.

Fritz-Meyer Sannon, PhD.

5 – They answered me angrily.

If, in other words, the adjective ends in **"e"** the **"e"** is dropped before adding **"-ly"**.

Examples:

1 – Simple – ***Simply***

2 – Subtle – ***Subtly***

3 – True – ***Truly***

4 – Capable – ***Capably***

5 – Gentle – ***Gently***

1 – She states it very simply to the staff.

2 – The artist works subtly on his masterpiece.

3 – I declare it truly to the judge.

4 – This teacher could do his job capably.

5 – My sister handles it gently to her supervisor.

Some adverbs of manner have the same form as the corresponding adjectives.

1 – *Fast* – **Fast**

2 – *Straight* – **Straight**

3 – *Hard* – **Hard**

4 – *Quick* – **Quick**

5 – *Slow* – **Slow**

1 – When I exercise in the morning, I walk fast.

2 – Go straight and you will find the post office.

3 – Mr. N. Williams works too hard.

4 – Do it as quick as you can.

5 – She walks too slow.

Note; The adjective **"quick"** and **"slow"** have two adverbs forms: **"Quick"** or **"quickly"**; **"slow"** or **"slowly"**.

G – Mid-sentence adverbs

Mid-sentence adverbs are adverbs that are placed in the middle of the sentence. They always precede the main verbs in present tense or in the past, and usually follow the verb to be. When there is a helping verb the mid-sentence adverb is placed between the helping verb and the main verb. The mid-sentence adverbs are:

1 – *Always*

2 – *Sometimes*

3 – *Extremely*

4 – *Often*

5 – *Never*

1 – I always arrive at school on time.

2 – She sometimes forgets to give her time sheet.

3 – Donna is extremely tired.

4 – She often asks for favors.

5 – She has never given up.

H – Adverbs of place

Adverbs of place are adverbs that tell us where things happen.

Examples:

1 – Anywhere

2 – Somewhere

3 – Here

4 – There

5 – Abroad *

1 – She is willing to go anywhere.

Do not confuse **"aboard" and **"abroad"**. Both are adverbs. **"Aboard"** means **in**, or **on the train, the bus, the plane**. Example: The American Airline crashed this morning, killing all the Dominicans aboard. **"Abroad"** means to or in a foreign country. Examples: My son lives abroad.*

2 – You will find your tools somewhere in the backyard.

3 – You could stay here.

4 – Go there, and you will see your bicycle.

5 – His girlfriend lives abroad.

I – Adverbs of probabilities

Adverbs of probabilities will tell us how frequently something happens.

They are:

1 – Perhaps

2 – Maybe

3 – Possible

4 – Probably

5 – Hopefully

1 – Perhaps I will go to the concert tonight.

2 – Maybe she did not receive our letter.

3 – I will probably go to Ponce.

4 – The other team will probably lose the game.

5 – Hopefully I will get there on time.

J – Adverbs of time

Adverbs of time tell us when something happens or happened. Here are some adverbs of time:

1 – Tomorrow

2 – Soon

3 – Yesterday

4 – Later

5 – Now

1 – The employees will get paid tomorrow.

2 – I will visit the place soon.

3 – Julio saw the teacher yesterday in Queens.

4 – My mother will buy the TV set later.

5 – I want to have it now.

K – Conjunctive adverbs

Conjunctive adverbs are adverbs that function like conjunctions. They are usually used to join clauses and are always followed by a comma. Here are some conjunctive adverbs:

1 – Consequently

2 – However

3 – Furthermore

4 – Accordingly

5 – Therefore

1 – She did not study at all; consequently, she fails the test.

2 – She is very clever; however, she is very lazy.

3 – She goes to Paris; furthermore, she will register for spring courses.

4 – The men robbed the bank; police acted accordingly.

5 – These workers work had; therefore, they receive a big check.

Exercises

Exercise A

<u>Put (ADE) after adverbs of degree and (ADU) after adverbs of duration if any</u>

1 – I have entirely finished with the project.

2 – She is totally correct.

3 – If you love me, why don't you marry me?

4 – Martha is allowed to use my computer indefinitely.

5 – When I see the sun, I feel much better.

6 – We enjoy the game immensely.

7 – Have you seen Khariyyha lately?

8 – You can stay in my house permanently.

9 – The doctor visited us very briefly.

10 – We strongly agree with Dr. Gordon.

Fritz-Meyer Sannon, PhD.

Exercise B

Underline the adverbs of emphasis where necessary

1 – I <u>certainly</u> want to buy the ticket.

2 – Please tell me your name.

3 – This is <u>positively</u> correct.

4 – When I am in Chicago, I feel <u>very</u> strange.

5 – I <u>really</u> enjoy the food.

6 – She works here temporarily.

7 – Tell me what you eat, I'll tell you what you are.

8 – Where are you going now?

9 – She was here <u>very</u> briefly.

10 – I am <u>absolutely</u> certain about that.

Exercise C

Underline all the adverbs of degree if any

1 – I <u>strongly</u> disagree with Mr. Ruddy.

2 – If you go there, tell him it is <u>totally</u> unacceptable.

3 – She covers immensely the whole area.

4 – Donna strongly believes in the teachings of Apostle John.

5 – She finished the whole job entirely.

6 – Dr. Gordon was totally in the right direction.

7 – State University/Queens EOC is adequately equipped.

8 – Today is a very cold day.

9 – She saw her dentist yesterday.

10 – She was totally wrong.

Exercise D

<u>Underline all the adverbs of duration if any</u>

1 – Linda is here temporarily.

2 – Are they going to be here indefinitely?

3 – Are they going to be here briefly.

4 – Let's make a deal now.

5 – Jesus Gonzalez loves the Mexican girl forever.

6 – I don't think you understand very well.

7 – She came in the hospital very briefly.

8 – Be quiet and let me talk now.

9 – Mrs. White certainly knows what she is doing.

10 – She has been here permanently.

Exercise E

<u>Indicate by putting (AF) after all the adverbs of frequency and (AM) after all the adverbs of manner</u>

1 – She sometimes goes to the movies with her son.

2 – She frequently visits her godmother.

3 – My little brother plays tennis well.

4 – My daughter is a fast driver.

5 – My wife frequently goes to PTA meetings.

6 – I have to ride with my son; she rides too fast.

7 – My mother knows how to drive perfectly.

8 – Do you really like to go to Ontario?

9 – She sometimes walks in the Park by herself.

10 – My fiancée does everything elegantly.

Exercise F

Underline all the adverbs of place if necessary

1 – Jesus lives in Bogota now.

2 – Give me money, a lot of money, I will teach you new tricks.

3 – I know there is a big church somewhere In Ottawa.

4 – My aunt works abroad; she is not here.

5 – My uncle does not live here any longer.

6 – Be quiet, you talk too much.

7 – Perhaps it is going to snow tonight.

8 – She does not live in Baranquilla anymore.

9 – I will see you later.

10 – The new couple lives now in Tegucigalpa.

Fritz-Meyer Sannon, PhD.

Exercise G

Underline all the adverbs of time if necessary.

1 – I will see you <u>tomorrow</u>.

2 – Mrs. Lateef would like to see Mr. Fritz <u>now</u>.

3 – See you <u>tomorrow</u>.

4 – Quebec is a beautiful city; my cousin lives there.

5 – I love you <u>forever</u>.

6 – Maria took the final exam <u>yesterday</u>.

7 – She simply wrote the words on a piece of paper.

8 – Bronx is one of the largest boroughs in New York City.

9 – I will see you <u>soon</u>; Irene will be there <u>soon</u>.

10 – Argentina is in big trouble <u>now</u>.

Exercise H

Fill in the appropriate conjunctive adverbs in the blank spaces

1 – She is very clever,……………., she is very lazy.

2 – Clara and Carmen did not study at all;………………, they did not pass the test.

3 – She was tired out;…………………, she could not go to work.

4 – Silvia studies every night;………………., she gets A+ for the final.

5 – We did not have any clue;………………., we found the place.

6 – I will go to the meeting;…………………, I will speak to him.

7 – I have money;………………. I will buy a house.

8 – Martino is very sick;……………….., he is going to play.

9 – The men robbed the bank; police acted………………,course.

10 – Mario is rich;……………….., he likes to beg in the street.

New English Grammar for ESL Students

Primitive farming method used by Andean farmers
Peru

Fritz-Meyer Sannon, PhD.

Chapter 9

What is a sentence?

Definition: A sentence is a unit of grammar that can stand alone. In other words, it is a group of words having a complete thought. A sentence begins with a capital letter, and ends with a period or full stop*; sometimes with a question mark or an exclamation point.

Examples:

    a) *I love my country.*

    b) *She went to California*

    c) *What is your real name?*

    d) *When she comes, tell her to wait for me.*

All the above examples are complete and real sentences; some of them are called *"major sentences"*, *"meaning sentences"* which contain one verb and one subject.

They left; some have three elements: I love you.

Besides the *"major sentences"* or real sentences there are *"incomplete sentences"*: sentences which cannot stand alone.

Such as:

   a) When you come later…

   b) Because she came too early…

   c) After you go…

The sentences (a,b,c) do not make any sense although they have a verb and a subject. They <u>are fragments of sentences</u> which we call "<u>clauses</u>" (see next chapter).

In modern American English, there are different types of sentences.

A) **Simple sentences**

B) **Compound sentences**

C) **Complex sentences**

D) **Compound-complex sentences**

E) **Declarative sentences**

Period: is American   *Full stop: is British*

F) **Imperative sentences**

G) **Interrogative sentences**

H) **Negative sentences**

I) **Exclamatory sentences**

J) **Conditional sentences**

K) <u>Simple sentences</u>

A simple sentence is a sentence with one subject, one finite verb. *Examples: She goes home. She eats well. She likes mangoes. John went to Peru.* The simple sentence is sometimes called independent clause (see chapter 10). The simple sentence does not have to have a direct object. Some verbs, called intransitive verbs do not have a direct object.

Examples: Birds fly.

God exists.

I agree.

"Birds fly." "God exists." "I agree." Are simple sentences or **"major sentences"**.

B. Compound sentences

A compound sentence is a sentence with two or more independent clauses, (not subordinate clauses) separated with one of the following coordinating conjunctions: **"and"**, **"or"**, **"but"**, **"for"**, **"so"**, **"yet"**.

Examples of compound sentences:

a) *Mrs. White goes to school and plays tennis.*

b) *Dora applied for the job and she got it.*

c) *I like my students and I respect them.*

d) *The students study hard and love the school.*

C) <u>Complex sentences</u>

A complex sentence is a sentence with a main clause* and one or more subordinate clauses.

Examples:

1 – Although my daughter is lazy, I love her.

2 – I will buy a car for Richard when he finishes high school.

3 – I study hard because I want to be a lawyer.

4 – If I were Liz, I would take more English classes.

Note*: A main clause is also called independent clause or principal clause. In the "New American English Grammar for ESL" main clause is used.

D) Compound-complex sentences

A compound-complex sentence is a sentence which contains two, three independent (or main) clause and at least one subordinate clause.

Examples:

1 – When my father was here, you spoke to him and asked him for money.

2 – If you come tomorrow, you will work for me and I will give you money.

3 – Even though it is raining, I will pick up Leonard and then I will go to school.

4 – If I were Liz, I would take more English classes and would study harder.

E) Declarative sentences

A declarative sentence is like a statement, which conveys information.

Such as:

1 – Fidel Castro has been in power since January 1959.

2 – I am proud to be a father.

3 – She is proud to be Puerto Rican.

4 – President Kennedy was a great president.

F) **Imperative sentences**

We use imperative sentences to give orders, issue requests, express commands.

Examples:

1 – Kiss your mother.

2 – Eat your food.

3 – Take your medicine.

4 – Get out from here.

English, as we know, is a S.V.O. language, meaning that the word order is: subject, verb and object. In the examples above: Kiss your mother; eat your food; take your medicine and get out from here, the subject is really "you", but it is not expressed; it is understood.

Kiss your mother – You kiss your mother

Eat your food – You eat your food.

Take your medicine – You take your medicine

Etc.

G) Interrogative sentences

We use interrogative sentences when we ask questions.

Examples: How old are you? Where do you live?

Sometimes, we use interrogative sentences not to seek information, but to give commands.

Examples:

- Could you close the door?

- Could you be quiet?

Note that interrogative sentences do not always refer to asking questions, or to giving orders as in the above examples. We usually use interrogative sentences for rhetorical purposes without expecting answer, or giving any orders.

Examples:

1) Do you think I am stupid?

2) What am I doing?

3) What is life?

H) Negative sentences

A negative sentence is the opposite of a positive sentence. A negative sentence expresses a negative idea like in the following examples:

1 – I don't like you.

2 – I don't understand anything.

3 – I know nothing.

4 – She is not smart.

I) **Exclamatory sentences**

An exclamatory sentence expresses feeling or strong emotions. It usually starts with **"what", "how", "ah"** and ends with an exclamation mark.

Examples:

1) How clever you are!

2) How cold it is!

3) What a nice day we have!

J) **Conditional sentences**

A conditional sentence is a sentence where one circumstance depends upon whether another circumstance exists. In the conditional sentence, there is always, one or more clauses "depending" on one or more other clauses introduced by **"if", or "when", or "unless",** etc. *Examples:*

1 – I will not give you the check unless you show me your time sheet.

2 – *When you come in, I will give you the key.*

3 – *If you study hard, you will pass the test.*

Conditional circumstances could be real, true, predictive, or speculative, meaning untrue contrary to the fact.

A) <u>True situation</u>

In true situations or scientific truth, the present tense is used in both fragments of the sentence.

Examples:

1) *If I don't eat, I get hungry.*

2) *If I have money, I buy books.*

3) *If it rains, the sidewalks are wet.*

B) <u>Predictive</u>

In a predictive situation, the present tense is used in the **"if"** clause or sometimes in the **"unless"** clause and the future tense is used in the main clause.

Fritz-Meyer Sannon, PhD.

Examples:

1 – If my fiancé comes tonight, he will bring me flowers.

2 – My mother will go home if my dad comes in.

3 – We will go to ESL III if we study hard.

Note that even though the verb in the **"if"** clause refers to an action in the future tense, the same rule applies.

Examples:

1) If Margarita comes tomorrow, I will explain everything to her.

2) I will do it for you, if you help me next Saturday.

3) I will cook this time if my wife comes tomorrow morning from Bogota.

C) <u>Untrue situation or not possible</u>.

According to the rule of <u>sequence of tenses</u>, when the verb in the "if" is in the past, we use the conditional **"would"**, **"might"**, or **"could"**.

Examples:

1) If I had the money, I would buy a house.

2) I could do it if you came.

3) She would go to Haiti if she received a lump sum check.

C^2) <u>Unreal situation-never occurred</u>

According to the same rule of **sequence of tenses**, when we speculate about something that never happened in the past, we use the past perfect in the "if" clause and the conditional perfect or past conditional in the main clause.

Examples: 1 – *I would have gone long time ago if she had told me that.*

2 – *If Alma had known that, she would have bought a piece of land in Puerto Plata.*

3 – *We would have been there if we had known.*

C³) Unreal situation/contrary to the fact

Sometimes we speculate about something which is untrue, that is impossible or totally contrary to the fact. In American English, we use **"if"** clause the verb to be in the subjunctive tense having the past tense form:

Singular: I were

You were

He, she were

Plural: We were

You were

They were

Examples:

1 – If Fritz were Nora, he would not do that.

2 – She could do a lot of things, if she were a man.

3 – If I were the President of the United State of America, I would give a big check to each student.

In fact, Fritz could not be Nora; that is something contrary to the fact because Fritz is a mature African-American man while Nora is a very young lady. (see example #1) In the example #3, I am not the President of the United States of America, because I am a professor. That is an unreal situation, contrary to the fact.

There are other conjunctions or expressions that express conditions in conditional sentences in addition to **"if"**. They are:

1 – Whether or not	6 – Even if
2 – In case of	7 – Providing (that)
3 – In the event that	8 – Provided (that)
4 – Unless	9 – Otherwise
5 – Only if	10 – Or else

Fritz-Meyer Sannon, PhD.

Examples:

1 – I am going to the movies by myself whether she comes or not.

2 – I will eat alone in case she does not show up.

3 – In the event that she does agree, I will sign the paper.

4 – I will not give a receipt unless you pay me first.

5 – I will go to the party only if my wife is invited.

6 – My cousin Lucia will go, even if it snows.

7 – Provided that you bring a note, I will accept you in class.

8 – I have to stop walking otherwise I get tired.

9 – You must surrender or (else) I shoot.

Remark I

Sometimes, it is possible to omit the conjunction **"if"** in the conditional sentence, the subject and verb inverted.

Examples:

1) If I were the King of England, I would give a check to everybody.

2) Had Alma known, she would have brought another house.

3) Should my son come, tell him to meet me at church.

Remark II

Sometimes the conjunction **"if"** is not expressed; it is understood, but the condition is implied.

Examples:

1 – She would have gone to Mexico with us, but she had to take the final on Friday.

2 – I would go with you with pleasure, but you came too late.

3 – I would buy a car, but I have no money.

Fritz-Meyer Sannon, PhD.

Remark III

Don't' Say	**Say**
If I will have money, I will go with you.	If I have money, I will go with you.
If I got rich, I will travel with you.	If I got rich, I would travel with you.
If I have a car, I would go with you.	If I have a car, I will go with you.
If I was you, I will share with the poor.	If I were you, I would share with the poor.
If my father was Chinese, he will teach me Chinese.	If my father were Chinese, he would teach me Chinese.

Exercises

Exercise A

Read the following very carefully and put *(CO)* after the complex sentences, *(in)* after the incomplete sentences and (comp) after the compound sentences

1 – If I were Jorge. (……)

2 – Although she is sick. (……)

3 – Today is Friday and tomorrow is Saturday. (……)

4 – Even though you're sick and you won't come, I love you. (……)

5 – I love you and I will marry you. (……)

6 – Marina is going to Columbia and will bring postal cards to the teacher. (……)

7 – After you finish your homework and clean your room, I will call you. (……)

8 – I will give you a lot of money if you fix the kitchen and paint the house. (……)

9 – When I see you. (…….)

10 – After you leave the room. (……)

Exercise B

<u>At the end of the following sentences, write *(in)* after the imperative sentences; *(neg)* after the negative sentences, and *(sim)* after the simple sentence</u>

1 – I am not going to the game tonight. (……)

2 – She loves me. (……)

3 – Be quiet. (……)

4 – Clara does not like codfish. (……)

5 – Take your medicine. (……)

6 – Please close the door. (……)

7 – I never stay too late outside. (……)

8 – Birds fly. (……)

9 – Queens EOC is a good school. (......)

10 – Let's go to the movies together. (......

Exercise C

Complete the following sentence with your own words

1 – If I knew

2 – We will buy a Toyota

3 – I would have bought

4 – You will buy a house

5 – Unless she comes on time

6 – If it doesn't rain

7 – We would stop coming

8 – We will buy it

9 – If she shows up

10 – If she were

Exercise D

Use the correct form in the blank space

1 – If you are rich, you……………give money to the poor.

2 – She……………..leave the room if the man came.

3 – If you…………… money, I will marry you.

4 – I………………wear an umbrella if it rains.

5 – My brother would have spoken to her is she……………….. (to want)

6 – She gets hungry if she…………………… (to eat)

7 – If you………………me, I like you.

8 – If my mother came, I………………..take her to dinner.

9 – I would give up if you…………………(to decide) to talk.

10 – If I won the lotto, I…………………buy a big house.

Exercise E

Use in place of the incorrect tense in the main clause.

1* - If I will be sick, I go to the doctor.

2* - Were I you, I will repeat the class.

3 – She knows that California is the largest states in the USA.

4* - After she comes, he would turn off the television.

5 – Paul doesn't think that Peter is really sick.

6* - I will buy a building in Manhattan if I won the lotto.

7 – Clara would buy a motorcycle if she has money.

8* - You get a promotion right away if you knew the right person.

9 – I knew she was here last night.

10* - If she would, she would.

Fritz-Meyer Sannon, PhD.

Exercise F

Replace the following **"if"** clauses by other words or expressions of condition and make the necessary changes if possible

*Incorrect

1 – If it is raining tomorrow, I won't go to the party.

2 – We would do it if you gave us the green light.

3 – I will give you your passport if you come early.

4 – You can go to any hospital if you have your Medicare card.

5 – If you dress up, I will welcome you in my house.

6 – If you have a tourist visa you cannot receive a SS check.

7 – You won't be eligible to apply if you are a legal alien.

8 – Julio will speak English if he comes to school.

9 – I will take my raincoat if it rains.

10 – If it stops raining, Juan will go to the party.

Exercise G

Complete the following sentences in the blank space by using your own word or expression of condition

1 – Dad would be very proud if

2 – If I were the president of the USA,

3 – My mother will be happy if

4 – The teacher will give a good grade if

5 – I could do it very well if

6 – Unless you leave the room

7 – If you know it,

8 – I will give you money if

9 – If she were queen, she

10 – She will marry me if

Exercise H

Change the following sentences, keeping the same condition without using "if" conjunction

1 – If I were you, I would change my hairstyle.

2 – She would go to Paris if she had money.

3 – I will go home if you come early.

4 – If you love me, kiss me.

5 – If someone should call, don't pick up the phone.

6 – She would dress up if she were Mrs. Leon.

7 – My wife will go there, if she has enough money.

8 – My mother would buy a bedroom if she had money.

9 – I would have bought it if I had know that.

10 – If I had known before, I would have told you.

New English Grammar for ESL Students

Winter in Quebec City
Canada
Mon Dieu! C'est terrible!

Fritz-Meyer Sannon, PhD.

Chapter 10

Parts of a sentence (continued)

The clause

Definition: A clause is a group of words having a subject and a predicate (a verb), but constitutes a fragment of a complex or compound sentence (see previous chapter). The independent is called a "simple sentence."

Example: Juan likes ice cream. It is a clause; it is an independent clause.

It is also a simple sentence. (See previous chapter part A)

There are different types of clauses:

A – Independent clauses

B – Main clauses

C – Subordinate clauses

1 – Subordinate clauses as adjective clauses

2 – Subordinate clauses as noun clauses

3 – Subordinate clauses as adverbial clauses such as: adverbial clauses of concession, of condition, of manner, etc.

A. <u>Independent clauses</u>

An independent clause is a clause (a group of words having at least a subject and a verb) which can stay alone without depending on another clause.

Examples: Today is a nice day.

a) State University, Queens EOC, is located in Jamaica, N.Y.

b) Hernst speaks English well.

Independent clauses are commonly called **"simple sentences"** (see chapter 9) because, as sentences, they are groups of words having a complete thought. *Ex. "Camilla* *eats oranges"* is an independent clause; it does not depend upon any other clause. *"Camilla eats oranges"* is also a simple sentence because it can stand alone and make sense.

B) Main Clauses

A main clause is a clause which can stand alone like the independent clause. The main clause has one verb, one subject. It is called: main clause, independent clause or principal clause. In "New English Grammar for ESL students" we define main clause as a clause on which another clause depends.

Example: Although today is Sunday, Antonio goes to school.

Antonio goes to school functions like an independent clause because it can stand alone but since another clause depends on it (Although today is Sunday), the subordinate clause or dependent clause, we call it main clause.

Fritz-Meyer Sannon, PhD.

Other examples:

1) If you come tomorrow, I will see you.

2) When you get in, turn on the television.

3) Since you are here, I will sign the contract.

4) I will marry you before you go to your country.

I will see you (#1) is the main clause because there is another clause depending on it.

Turn on the television (#2) is the main clause because there is another clause depending on it.

I will sign the contract (#3) is the main clause because there is another clause depending on it.

I will marry you (#4) is the main clause because there is another clause depending on it.

C) **Subordinate clauses**

Subordinate clauses are fragments of sentences; they have subjects and verbs, sometimes direct and/or

indirect objects. They cannot stand alone and depend on other clauses: the main clauses. They don't make sense because they are incomplete. Subordinate clauses usually begin with subordinate conjunctions, such as: after, before, if, since, unless, when, while, because, etc. or relative pronouns. *("that", "who", "whom", "whose",* **"which".)**

Since the subordinate clauses depend on other clauses they function as nouns, as adjectives and as adverbs.

1) <u>Subordinate clauses as adjective clauses</u>

The adjective clauses have the function of adjectives; they describe or modify nouns and pronouns; in other words, they give information about nouns or pronouns. They are usually introduced by relative pronouns *("whose", "that", "which",* etc.). Adjective clauses are also called relative clauses.

Fritz-Meyer Sannon, PhD.

Examples: 1 – This is the man whose wife is in the hospital.

2 – The cat that is there is mine.

3 – That is the car which I want to buy.

ESL students have to remember that they can change an adjective clause to and adjective phrase (see adjective phrase chapter 11) by eliminating the relative pronoun and by changing the verb form.

Examples: 1 – The boy who came this morning is very smart.

The boy coming this morning is very smart.

2 – Anybody who wants to buy my house is really rich.

Anybody wanting to buy my house is really rich.

3 – The lady who is sitting there is my fiancée.

The lady sitting there is my fiancée.

4 – The cat that is under the table is too ugly.

The cat under the table is too ugly.

5 – *The toys which are on that shelf are very expensive.*

The toys on that shelf are very expensive.

2) **Subordinate clauses as noun clauses**

Nouns have two functions; they are either subjects or objects.

Examples:

a) *Paul lives on the first floor.* **Paul** *is a proper noun.* **Paul** *is the subject of the verb lives.*

b) *They saw the man;* **man** *is the object of the verb saw. A noun clause performs in a sentence a function similar to a noun. A noun clause acts as the subject, object or complement of a main clause. A main clause is also called a nominal clause.*

Most of the noun clauses begin with question words such as **what, where, why, which, when** or conjunctions, **whether** or **if** etc.

Examples: Noun clauses as subjects

1 – What you say doesn't make sense.

2 – When Nora arrives is unimportant to me.

3 – What he just bought us is very expensive.

Noun clauses as objects:

1 – I don't like what you say.

2 – She doesn't know when he will propose.

3 – I don't know whether she will come or not.

3) <u>Subordinate clauses as adverbial clauses</u>

Adverbial clauses are subordinate or dependent clauses; we can put them before the main clause.

Example: When you want to come, call me up or after the main clause: Call me up when you want to come.

As adverbial clauses they modify the main clauses by giving information or details about:

Concession

Condition

Manner

Place

Purpose

Result

Reason

a) <u>Adverbial clauses of concession</u>

Adverbial clauses of concession are also called adverbial clauses of opposition because they contain facts that are contrary to the situations expressed in the main clauses. They are usually introduced by subordinating conjunctions **although, even though, though, whereas, while.**

Examples:

Fritz-Meyer Sannon, PhD.

*1 – He passed the class **even though** he has many absences.*

*2 – **While** he stays home, I am going to Central Park.*

*3 – **Though** it is snowing, I am going to work.*

*4 – He lives in Santiago **whereas** his wife lives in Santo Domingo.*

*5 – **Although** Yolanda resides in Boston, I will marry her.*

b) Adverbial clauses of condition

Adverbial clauses of condition are subordinating clauses dealing with possible sometimes impossible situations (situations contrary to the facts, or unreal situations). The adverbial clauses of condition are introduced by the conjunction: "**if**" (and they are called **"if"** clauses); they are also introduced by other conjunctions: **Unless, providing (that), produced (that), as long as,** etc. *Examples:*

1 – If you clean up today, I will take you to New York.

2 – I would give you money, if you had it.

3 – *If she were a senator, she would vote in favor of bilingual education.*

4 – *As long as you have a valid passport, you can travel.*

5 – *Providing that you pay, you will be invited.*

6 – *Unless you bring a doctor's note, I will not accept you.*

c) Adverbial clauses of manner

Adverbial clauses of manner are subordinating clauses that describe how things are done. They are usually introduced by conjunction or expressions such as:

As,

As if,

As though,

Like,

etc.

Examples:

1 – *He acts strangely as if he is very stupid.*

2 – She looks at the gentlemen as if she loves him.

3 – He walks on the sidewalk as though he is drunk.

4 – No one could do it like he did it.

d) <u>Adverbial clauses of place</u>

Adverbial clauses of place are subordinate clauses that show or indicate place or location of an action. The adverbial clauses are usually introduced by the conjunction:

where, everywhere, wherever, etc.

1 – Wherever he is, he is a funny guy.

2 – They will find him wherever he is.

3 – Everywhere he goes, he becomes a troublemaker.

4 – Where you lead, I will follow.

5 – I will go wherever you want to go.

e) **Adverbial clauses of purpose**

Adverbial clauses of purpose are subordinating clauses referring to the purpose or intention of or a person when doing something. The adverbial clauses of purpose are introduced by the conjunctions or expressions:

To,

So,

So that,

In order to

Examples:

1 – She talks in class just to upset the teacher.

2 – Alma works hard in order to save money.

3 – My mother turned off the light in order to save electricity.

F) **Adverbial clauses of result**

Adverbial clauses of result are subordinating clauses which – as the name indicates – refer to the result of an event and are introduced by:

So,

So that.

Examples:

1 – She didn't study enough, so she failed the test.

2 – She was running in the park so fast that she got tired and became sick.

g) **Adverbial clauses of cause and effect**

Adverbial clauses of cause and effect are subordinating clauses that explain the reason, an event or situation. They are also called adverbial clauses of reason and are introduced by:

Because,

As,

Since,

Now that,

As/so long as,

Inasmuch as.*

Examples:

1 – I don't like you because you are too mean.

Since you didn't come, I couldn't give it to you.

2 – As you have nothing to say, I can't forgive you.

As you have no money, you can't buy the car.

3 – Since today is Sunday, I will go to church.

I will not go to school, since today is a holiday.

4 – Now that you broke the law, you will be punished.

I cannot marry you now that you return my ring.

5 – As long as you are here, you have to wait.

You can buy the house as long as you have money.

6 – The summit meeting was postponed for next week inasmuch as there were riots all day.

The coup d'Etat was a big fiasco **"inasmuch"** as the leaders of the opposition could not reach an agreement.

*"**inasmuch**" as is rarely used; in formal situation with the meaning of "because", but "because" is commonly used.

<u>Remark</u>: The subordinating clauses or adverbial clauses precede or follow the main clauses, and the meaning does not change.

Examples:

a) *Because she came late, she did not catch the plane.*

b) *She did not catch the plane because she arrived late.*

There is no difference in meaning but when the adverbial precedes the main clause, it is important to put a comma at the end of the adverbial clause.

Exercises

Exercise A

Underline all the independent clauses in the following where necessary.

1 – Since you are rich, you own many cars.

2 – Quebec is a beautiful city.

3 – My father is very sick.

4 – Dominican Republic is a beautiful country.

5 – Yesterday was Friday.

6 – If you won the lotto, I would be happy.

7 – The first day of the week is Sunday.

8 – Although you are smart I win anyway.

9 – Give me one dollar and I will give you ice cream.

10 – My daughter is very sick.

11 – After you got here, we'll go.

Exercise B

Underline all the main clauses in the following sentences if any

1 – <u>I am happy</u> when you are.

2- <u>She got the time</u> and <u>she got the money</u>.

3 – Although you are strong and healthy, <u>you caught a cold</u>.

4 – <u>My mother bought a big house</u> because she had money.

5 – <u>The students of the University of Montreal are very bright</u>.

6 – If she were the teacher, <u>she would give homework everyday</u>.

7 – <u>She went to California</u> and <u>he went to Atlanta</u>.

8 – <u>My mother and my father are both senior citizens</u>.

9 – When Maria comes in, <u>tell her to start dinner</u>.

10 – Since she came early, <u>she obtained everything</u>.

11 – <u>Jose went to the hospital</u> since he was sick.

Exercise C

Underline all the subordinating clauses in the following sentences where necessary

1 – <u>If you want to go</u>, tell me now.

2 – <u>After she read the paper to me</u>, I agreed the Mayor was right.

3 – <u>When you close a school</u>, you open a prison.

4 – After Monday is Tuesday.

5 – Give me love.

6 – <u>Although Acapulco is beautiful</u>, I prefer Mexico City.

7 – <u>If today is Monday</u>, tomorrow will be Tuesday.

8 – Yale University and Columbia University are good schools.

9 – <u>Since Mario is not a US citizen</u>, he cannot vote.

10 – A friend in need is a friend indeed.

11 – <u>When you are tired</u>, take a nap.

Fritz-Meyer Sannon, PhD.

Exercise D

Indicate by **(#1)** all the independent clauses; indicate **(#2)** all the main clauses and by **(#3)** all the adjective clauses.

1 – My brother is very healthy.

2 – Queens EOC is a very good school.

3 – My brother-in-law bought a new Mercedes because he is rich.

4 – Today is Sunday.

5 – Please help me.

6 – I wouldn't do it if you asked.

7 – Stand up and say "Good Morning" to Mr. George.

8 – The man who is in my house is a detective.

9 – Even though Mario is sick, he goes swimming.

10 –If you go there, I will go too.

11 – The roach which is in the soup is big.

Exercise E

Underline all the adjective clauses in the following sentences

Ex. The boy <u>who came</u> today is crazy.

1 – Queens EOC <u>which is located in New York</u> is a good institution.

2 – The boy <u>who is here</u> is crazy.

3 – Donna and Camilla <u>who were at the party yesterday</u> became sick.

4 – The man <u>who lives there</u> is a singer.

5 – Who laughs today will cry tomorrow.

6 – A swallow does not make a summer.

7 – Leopold Sedar Seugher died at the age of 95.

8 – Thank God today is Friday.

9 – My aunt is a nurse.

10 – Mr. William <u>whom I spoke to</u> won 25 million dollars.

11 – Mr. Fritz who is our teacher goes on vacation.

Exercise F

Write (NC) after all noun clauses and (AC) after all adjective clauses.

Ex. What you said is not true. The cat which is under the table.

    (NC)   (AC)

1 – I like what you said.

2 – The book which is on my desk is a very good book.

3 – The merchant who came today is from Bangladesh.

4 – I don't appreciate what you have done.

5 – Tell me what you eat and I will tell you what you are.

6 – San Juan which is the Capital of Puerto Rico is beautiful.

7 – Peru that is located in South America is very beautiful.

8 – My car which is over there is a very expensive car.

9 – All you say is not important to me.

10 – I love what I see tonight.

11 – What you said is very stupid.

Exercise G

In the adverbial clauses of purposes use the appropriate subordinate conjunctions in the space provided.

1 – I want to study ………………….pass the test.

2 – This country is making weapons…………………win the war.

3 – Our teacher gave us a quiz………………….give us evaluation.

4 – My wife saves a lot of money…………………….buy a house.

5 – My adviser gives me a bad evaluation…………………push me to do better.

6 – My husband gives me money…………………..buy toys for Christmas.

7 – My uncle works had……………………..get more money.

8 – My children go to the park…………………..play basketball.

9 – Joseph Stalin sent his secretary to Siberia……………..keep secret after meeting with Ch. De Gaulle.

10 – My brother runs everyday ……………… be the winner.

11 – You have to eat…………………..live.

Exercise H

In place of the conjunction "because", use other conjunctions such as **"since"**, **"inasmuch as"**, **"as long as"**, **"as"**, **"now that"**, etc. in the following adverbial clauses.

1 – Because you love me, why don't you marry me?

2 – I will go to Peru because my wife is there.

3 – I cannot get good flowers because this is not the season.

4 – Because there are problems in Argentina I stay in NY.

5 – I will marry you because I love you very much.

6 – I won't need food because I just ate.

7 – Because it is raining I wont' go swimming.

8 – I buy your car because it is a good car.

9 – The meeting was cancelled because the weather was bad.

10 – I will not play tonight because I am sick.

11 – Because you are here, I will invite you.

Fritz-Meyer Sannon, PhD.

16th century ruin in Old Panama
Panama

Fritz-Meyer Sannon, PhD.

Chapter 11

Parts of a Sentence (continued)

The Phrase

Definition: a phrase (from Latin Phrasis) is a group of words having no verb, no subject. There are different types of phrases. *Ex. Under the stairs, after the meeting, since yesterday morning.*

There are different kinds of phrases:

A – **Appositive phrases**

B – **Gerund phrases**

C – **Infinitive phrases**

D – **Noun phrases**

E – **Participial phrases**

F – **Prepositional phrases**

Fritz-Meyer Sannon, PhD.

G – **Verbal phrases**

H – **Adjective phrases**

<u>A – **Appositive phrases**</u>

Appositive phrases have nothing in common with **"clauses"** or **"sentences",** they have no verbs, no subjects. They function like adjectives, but unlike adjectives they don't describe or modify; they are in apposition to nouns or pronouns meaning they rename the subjects (or objects) they are equivalents.

Examples:

1) *Napoleon Bonaparte <u>1st Consul in France</u>, sent Captain Leclerc to Saint Domingue.*

2) *Pauline Bonaparte, <u>Napoleon's sister</u>, married Captain Leclerc.*

3) *Toussaint Louverture, <u>Governor of Saint Domingue</u>, died April 7, 1803 in Fort de Joux in France.*

All the underlined groups of words or phrases: "1st Consul in France", "Napoleon Bonaparte's sister", "governor of Saint Domingue" are appositive phrases. They don't describe or modify the nouns or subjects. Since there are subjects already. They are in apposition to the subjects.

B – Gerund phrases

The gerund phrases are groups of words having no verbs, no subjects. The gerund phrases function as nouns meaning they are either subjects or objects (of complements of prepositions.)

1 – *Running everyday* is good for our health.

2 – *Speaking a foreign language in class* is not permitted.

3 – *Eating in the morning* is very important.

4 – I don't like *playing in the backyard*.

5 – I love *running everyday*.

Fritz-Meyer Sannon, PhD.

All the underlined phrases are gerund phrases: They function as nominals.

For instance:

1 – <u>Running everyday</u> is the subject of is good...

2 – <u>Speaking a foreign language</u> is the subject of is not permitted.

3 – <u>Eating in the morning</u> is the subject of is very important.

4 – <u>Playing in the backyard</u> is the direct object of like.

5 – <u>Running everyday</u> is the direct object of love.

Do not confuse the present participle and the gerund although both have the same form of "*ing*".

1 – She hates **<u>drawing</u>** with markers. (*"Drawing" is gerund, because it is object*)

2 – Avoid <u>speaking</u> too loud. (*"Speaking" is gerund; because it is object*)

3 – They were **<u>playing</u>** basketball. (***Present** participle*)

C – Infinitive phrases

The infinitive phrases start with infinitives, that is to say **"to"** + the basic form of the verb like with: **"to go"**, **"to sleep"**, **"to take"**, **"to swim"**, etc. The infinitive phrases can have the functions of adjectives (modifying or describing nouns or pronouns) or the functions of nouns (subject or objects of the verb) or the functions of adverbs (modifying verbs, adverbs, or adjectives).

Examples:

*1 – I have a jacket **to clean now**. (modify or describe)*

*2 – Xiomara carries the flag **to give to** the teacher. (describe)*

*3 – This is the room **to paint** today. (modify or describe)*

*1 – I would like **to go** home early. (object)*

*2 – **To eat well** is a very good sign. (subject)*

*3 – Benoit likes **to see the baby birds**. (object)*

1 – *She drives too fast **to brake on** the corner.*

2 – *It is too cold **to go out** today.*

3 – *It's too hot **to drink it all at once**.*

D – Noun phrases

Nouns can have two functions: subject or objects.

Paul is smart; Antonio walks fast.

or Sonia loves Romero; The rat bites Regine.

In the above examples Paul is a noun, he is the subject of is. Antonio is a noun, he is the subject of walks. Sonia is a noun, she is the subject of loves and Romero is the object of loves. Rat is a noun, it is the subject of bites and Regine is a noun, she is the object of bites.

As we can see, nouns can be subjects or objects. Noun phrases refer to a group of words having no verb, no real subject and function like nouns in a sentence.

Examples:

*1 – **<u>Some African children</u>** are very poor.*

*2 – **<u>Spanish women</u>** are very good cooks.*

*3 – I love **<u>those strong figthers.</u>***

*4 – **<u>The French Parisian women</u>** are smart.*

*5 – My mother bought a **<u>four-bedroom ranch</u>**.*

<u>Some African children</u> is the subject of are.

<u>Spanish women</u> is the subject of are.

<u>Those strong fighters</u> are the object of love.

<u>The French Parisian women</u> are the subject of are.

<u>A four-bedroom ranch</u> is the object of bought.

<u>E – Participial phrases</u>

Participial phrases contain present participles or past participles and function like adjectives: they modify nouns.

Fritz-Meyer Sannon, PhD.

A) **Present participial phrases**

Present participial phrases contain a present participle in the phrases; they modify the nouns or pronouns.

Examples:

1 – **Now having a lot of money**, he plans to go to Quito.

2 – **Eating everyday on time** is the best medicine.

3 – **While dancing happily** my wife got good news.

4 – **Being a good artist** is not a common thing.

5 – **Walking all day long**, Carmen wants a drink.

B) **Past participial phrases**

Past participial phrases contain a past participle in the phrase; they modify the nouns or pronouns.

Examples:

1 – **Gone home very** sad is not a good sign.

2 – **Convicted three times**, he has no remorse.

3 – **Written quickly**, the note is illegible.

4 – ***Bought in a small town***, this car is very strong.

5 – ***Arrested twice the same day***, Joseph looks pale.

F – Prepositional phrases

Prepositional phrases contain prepositions and can function as adjectives modifying nouns or pronouns, as adverbs modifying adjectives, verbs or other adverbs. Prepositional phrases beginning with the prepositions on, of, with, etc. usually end with nouns or pronouns.

Examples:

1 – On the desk

2 – On the big table

3 – For us

4 – From us

5 – With pleasure

6 – With a lot of courage

Fritz-Meyer Sannon, PhD.

In this way, the noun or pronoun is the object of the preposition.

1 – Desk complement of on

2 – Table complement of on

3 – Us complement of for

4 – Us complement of from

5 – Please complement of with

6 – Courage complement of with

Prepositional phrases can modify nouns, pronouns, or modifying adjectives, verbs or other adverbs.

Examples:

1 – The boy dresses **_in a blue shirt_**. *(modifying boy)*

2 – The woman goes out **_with a yellow blouse_**. *(modifying woman)*

3 – My father doesn't like to see her **_with that guy_**. *(modifying her)*

4 – My mother likes him **in his new shirt**. *(modifying him)*

5 – Fritz plays **in the basement**. *(modifying plays)*

6 – She works **at McDonald's**. *(modifying works)*

7 – I feel really good **in the morning**. *(modifying good)*

8 – Isabel is always sick **in winter**. *(modifying sick)*

9 – She dances well **with her partner**. *(modifying well)*

10 – She studies hard **for the test**. *(modifying hard)*

G – Verbal phrases

What do we mean by verbal phrases?

Phrases – as we have already known – are groups of words having no verbs.

Phrases could not be nonverbal or verbal.

Nonverbal phrases are phrases that do not contain verbs such as:

1 – Noun phrases: **The tall lady is German**

2 – Prepositional phrases: **Under the stairs**.

3 – Appositive phrases: **Pauline, sister of Napoleon Bonaparte**.

4 – Adjective phrases: **The man sitting there is drunk**.

Verbal phrases are phrases that have verbals (verb form) that do not function as verbs of the clauses. They can be objects, complements, modifiers, etc.

1 – **Participial phrases** are phrases that have verbals (participles present, past) that do not function as verbs.

Example: Eating too much, Pedro becomes obese.

2 – **Gerund phrases** are phrases that have verbals (gerund) that do not functions as verbs.

Example: Walking in the snow is not a good thing to do.

3 – **Infinitive phrases** are phrases that have verbals (infinitive) that do not function as verbs.

Example: To be strong and healthy is my ambition.

H – Adjective phrases

Adjective phrases are groups of words that do not contain verbs and subjects. Adjective phrases modify nouns.

Example:

1 – The man **at the corner** is my friend.

2 – The car **on the street** is my wife's car.

3 – The tie **in the closet** is very expensive.

4 – The pencil **on the desk** is mine.

5 – The teacher **with the blue shirt** is very tough.

As you can notice almost all the adjective phrases are also prepositional phrases:

Examples:

1 – **At the corner** is an adjective phrase because it describes the man. At the same time at the corner is a nonverbal phrase, a prepositional phrase because it starts with the preposition **"at"**.

2 – **On the street** is an adjective phrase because it describes the car. At the same time on the street is a nonverbal phrase, prepositional phrase because it starts with the preposition "**on**".

3 – **In the closet** is an adjective phrase because it describes the tie. At the same time, in the closet is a nonverbal phrase, a prepositional phrase because it starts with the preposition "*in*".

4 – **On the desk** is an adjective phrase because it describes the pencil (not any pencil, but the pencil on the desk). At the same time on the desk is a nonverbal phrase, a prepositional phrase it starts with the preposition "**on**".

5 – **With the blue shirt** is an adjective phrase because it describes the teacher (not any teacher, but the teacher with the blue shirt). At the same time with the blue shirt is a

nonverbal phrase, a prepositional phrase because it starts with the preposition **'with"**.

Note: Do not confuse phrases, clauses and sentences. ESL students sometimes get mixed up because in French and in Spanish "phrase", "frase" mean sentences.

Remember: A <u>phrase</u> is a group of words having no verb, no subject; whereas a <u>clause</u> is a group of words having at least one verb and one subject. A <u>sentence</u>, on the contrary is a group of words having a complete sense.

1 – *Under the table.* (phrase)

2 – *After tomorrow morning.* (phrase)

1 – `After you come in.` *(clause)*

2 – `When you will see it.` (clause)

1 – *If you come, I will take you to Rockefeller Center.* (sentence)

2 – *Even though you don't have a degree, I love you.* (sentence)

A clause could be also a sentence, a simple sentence. Example: **I love you**, is a clause because it has one verb, one subject. **"I love"** you is also a sentence because it has a complete thought.

But the phrase has no verb at all (meaning finite verb) and doesn't have a complete thought.

Examples:

1 – Because of your laziness. (phrase)

2 – After July 1. (phrase)

3 – Before Sunday afternoon. (phrase)

Exercises

Exercise A

Put (PH) after all phrases and (CL) after all clauses

1 – My father and my mother went to church.

2 – Nelson and her brother have money.

3 – Take my clothes and my toys.

4 – When you see the teacher, tell him to go to the office.

5 – If she were a teacher, she would give homework everyday.

6 – After the game, go home.

7 – After you finish, see me in the office.

8 – Since you are busy, call me tomorrow.

9 – Because you have money, I will pray for you.

10 – A friend in need is a friend indeed.

11 – All the students go to the library.

12 – If I win the lotto, I would give you one million dollars.

Exercise B

<u>Underline all noun phrases once, underline all noun clauses twice</u>

1 – John and Mary went to the movie together.

2 – My sister-in-law is very happy.

3 – Shut up the big heavy door.

4 – She carries two leaves of palm crosswise to indicate she has visited the Holy Land.

5 – Nora, Jose, Liz are good students.

6 – She picks up everything on the floor.

7 – I love you because you love me.

8 – If she were the Queen, she would travel around the world.

9 – I have been thinking of you since I saw you today.

10 – Because of your courage, I admire you.

11 – Since this morning, I have been thinking of you.

12 – When I see you, I feel happy.

Exercise C

Underline the adjective phrases where necessary

1 – Give me the hat on the shelf.

2 – I don't know the man in the book store.

3 – I see the boy with a lot of tattoos.

4 – The policemen at the station is from El Salvador.

5 – Have a nice day.

6 – I will give money to the man in the living room.

7 – The dictionary under the desk is Regine's.

8 – The car in the garage is hers.

9 – The car which is the garage is too old.

10 – The man with a blue shirt is crazy.

Exercise D

Write (NP) after all noun phrases in the following sentences

1 – The beautiful house over there is mine.

Fritz-Meyer Sannon, PhD.

2 – I don't appreciate your lousy job.

3 – Do you see the big consequences?

4 – Come to me after the break.

5 – Since you don't see, I won't show you.

6 – All that story is garbage.

7 – My little brother is not responsible.

8 – Her long experience is not enough.

9 – Call me Dad, I will take care of you.

10 – Christine eats a lot of plantains.

1 – I will call you up after midnight.

2 – To live a good life is difficult.

3 – After the game, I will meet my friend.

4 – Under the roof, there is a dead cat.

5 – I want to see you soon.

6 – Pierre has to meet Marina before 8 o'clock.

7 – I will do it with your green light.

8 – To run in the morning is the best medicine.

9 – I have been waiting for you since yesterday.

Exercise H

Write (APP) after the appositive phrases, (GE) after the gerund phrases and (NN) after noun phrases where necessary

1 – I don't like eating in the morning.

2 – The Dominican women are good dressmakers.

3 – Walking on the sidewalk.

4 – Raul Castro is a tough soldier.

5 – Doing the right thing is the secret of life.

6 – Fritzy Brown is the assistant principal of that High School.

7 – Eating early morning is healthy.

8 – I love Columbian women.

9 – I would like to speak to Mrs. Lateef, director of Queens EOC.

10 – The old man is really sick.

Exercise E

<u>Write all prepositional phrases underneath the following sentences</u>

1 – You will see it on the big desk.

2 – Before seven o'clock, everything will be OK.

3 – Before you come in, call me please.

4 – Tell me what you eat I will tell you what you are.

5 – Inasmuch as the leaders didn't agree, the meeting was cancelled.

6 – Since you are so lazy, I won't take you to the park.

7 – When you come in, turn off the light.

8 – Come in after 8 o'clock.

9 – I usually wake up at 7 o'clock.

10 – Even though you don't agree with me…

11 – I have been cooking since this morning.

Exercise F

<u>Complete the following sentences by using the prepositional phrases in the blank spaces</u>

1 – She places the book……………………. .

2 – On………………………..I will start exercising.

3 – I have been studying English…………………….

4 - …………………….I will marry you.

5 -…………………….I don't marry you.

6 – I will be today………………………..

7 – My cousin went…………………….during vacation.

8 – I have to be there…………………………..

9 - …………………….please call me.

10 – I have been waiting for you…………………….

11 -…………………….I will stop smoking.

12 – My mother went to buy breakfast .

Exercise G

Underline all the prepositional phrases and underline twice all the verbal phrases

1 – To recite a prayer each morning helps a lot.

2 – I will call you up after midnight.

3 – To live a good life is difficult.

4 – After the game, I will meet my friend.

5 – Under the roof, there is a dead cat.

6 – I will do it with your green light.

7 – To run in the morning is the best medicine.

Exercise H

Write (APP) after the appositive phrase, (GE) after the gerund phrase and (NN) after the noun phrase where necessary.

1 – I don't like eating in the morning.

2 – Walking on side walk.

3 – Raoul Castro, brother of Fidel, is a tough soldier.

4 – I love Haïtian women.

5 – What a beautiful day is today.

6 – George W. Bush, President of the United States of America, is in good health.

Fritz-Meyer Sannon, PhD.

New English Grammar for ESL Students

Office Building
Place de l'Independance
Dakar, Senegal
(Africa)

Fritz-Meyer Sannon, PhD.

Chapter 12

Object Completing Element

Definition: English is (like many languages) a S.V.O. language meaning: **subject**, **verb**, **object**. Not all languages are S.V.O. languages. Some languages are O.V.S. or V.S.O. but the word order in English is **subject**, **verb**, **object**. Examples: *The cats eat the rats.*

The cats are subjects.

Eat is the verb.

Rats are objects.

Almost all verbs have subjects and objects.

| John | drinks | water |
| Subject | Verb | Object |

Fritz-Meyer Sannon, PhD.

A. The verbs which have objects (precisely direct objects) are called transitive verbs. *Examples:*

    *Buy a **book***

    *Take a **book***

    *See the **movie***

    *Write a **book***

    *Cash a **check***

As you have seen, the direct object could be a noun like house, book, movie, check.

B. The direct object could be a noun phrase

(Noun phrase is a group of words with no verb, no subject having the function of object.)

Examples:

1 – Alma has seen the **old Spanish church**.

2 – Rosario bought **a very beautiful ranch**.

3 – Alexandra and Martha **like expensive red flowers**.

4 – Jarin bought **_a lot of big toys._**

5 – Fritz knows **_all the big cities in Canada_**.

C. The direct object could be a noun clause

(Noun clause is a group of words with at least a finite verb and a subject having the function of object of the verb.)

1 – I don't understand **what you said**.

2 – I tell you **what will happen**.

3 – He said **that he would be home by Christmas**.

4 – Olga does not want **what she did not ask for.**

5 – I love **when you smile**.

D. The direct object could be a pronoun

A pronoun is a word that takes the place of a noun. The pronoun is the direct object of the verb. The pronoun could be

1 – A personal pronoun object

    a) I love **her**

    b) She loves **me**

    c) We like **them**

2 – A demonstrative pronoun

    a) I like **that**

    b) Silvia picks **this**

    c) She loves **those**

3 – A possessive pronoun

    a) Walter buys **yours**

    b) I prefer **hers**

    c) They don't like **mine**

4 – or an indefinite pronoun

    a) Blanca wants to bring **somebody**

    b) I will accept **everyone**

    c) I don't want **anything**

E. Some English verbs have no direct object. They cannot be followed by an object. They call them **intransitive verbs**. Verbs like:

1 – **agree**

2 – **exist**

3 – **sleep**

4 – **go**

5 – **stay**

I – I agree with you. (**Agree** what? No answer. No direct object.)

2 – God exists. (**Exists** what? No answer. No direct object.)

3 – Nooria sleeps too much. (**Sleeps** what? No answer. No direct object)

4 – Nishat went to Miami. (**Went** what? No answer. No direct object)

5 – I stay home on Sunday. (**Stay** what? No answer. No direct object)

F. Some other verbs could be transitive or intransitive at the same time

Verbs such as:

1 – **Speak**

2 – **study**

3 – **grow**

4 – **smell**

5 – **taste**

1 – Bonilla would like to speak to me. (intransitive)

1 – Most of the people who live in Montreal speak French. (transitive)

2 – The Queens EOC students study hard. (intransitive)

2 – The students study their lessons. (transitive)

3 – What do you want to be when you grow up? (intransitive)

3 – They grow corn in the South. (transitive)

4 – The man smells very bad. (intransitive)

4 – Why do you have to smell the bread? (transitive)

5 – The orange tastes sour. (intransitive)

5 – The baby tastes the food. (transitive)

G. Objects of a preposition

We already said in paragraph C that the direct object could be a noun clause. Now, remember that the object could be a prepositional phrase, and the object of the preposition is a noun or pronoun. Some prepositions are the following:

1 – in

2 – at

3 – to

4 – under

Fritz-Meyer Sannon, PhD.

5 – on

1 – The New York State employees eat **in the cafeteria**.

2 – The guys play **in the backyard**.

3 – I want to go **to a good college**.

4 – My cousin put his hat **under the big table**.

5 – Don't hesitate, put your jacket **on the chair**.

Ref #1 – **In the cafeteria** is a prepositional phrase introduced by the preposition **"in." Cafeteria** is the object of the preposition **"in."**

Ref #2 – **In the backyard** is a prepositional phrase, introduced by the preposition **"in." Backyard** is the object of the preposition **"in."**

Ref #3 – **To a good college** is a prepositional phrase, introduced by the preposition **"to." College** is the object of the preposition **"to."**

Ref #4 – **Under the big table** is a prepositional phrase, introduced by the preposition **"under."** Table is the object of the preposition **"under."**

Ref #5 – **On the chair** is a prepositional phrase, introduced by the preposition **"on." Chair** is the object of the preposition **"on."**

H – Objects of a Verbal (or verbals as objects)

In addition to direct object, indirect object, noun phrase object, noun clause object, pronoun object, object of preposition, English has objects of a verbal or verbal objects. Verbals could also be nominals.

1 – Stop talking in class.

2 – Keep doing the same thing.

3 – I'd like to ask you a favor.

4 – Do you want to go there?

Fritz-Meyer Sannon, PhD.

Exercises

Exercise A

Underline all the transitive verbs and put (TV) after all transitive verbs

1 – Jean Paul bought a Honda 2003.

2 – Harold gave flowers to Anita.

3 – Tell me your last name, please.

4 – My uncle Balaguer bought me a television set.

5 – I asked you a big favor; did you hear me?

Exercise B

Indicate all the intransitive verbs and write (IV) after them

1 – Today is not a good day.

2 – My friend went to Paris last year.

3 – If you have money, why don't you go to Mexico.

4 – I would buy you a building if I won the lotto.

5 – Let me tell you: "I love you."

6 – After you finish call em.

7 – When you go there, buy me perfume.

8 – Believe it or not, I don't understand.

9 – My parents have three cars.

10 – Could you tell me where family court is?

11 – She wants me to leave the house.

12 – He gave her a Toyota on her birthday.

Exercise C

Indicate all the pronouns objects. Underline them

1 – I love those.

2 – Be quiet and listen to me.

3 – Poor John, he didn't understand that.

4 – Is this true you like him?

5 – No, I don't like him at all?

6 – Give me your picture, I will give you mine.

7 – If you see her, tell her hello.

8 – I don't know anything.

Exercise D

Underline all the noun clause objects in the following

1 – My friend has received <u>what she asked for</u>.

2 – Irene did not expect <u>what she was</u>.

3 – How do you like to go with them?

4 – Yolanda is very smart; she understood <u>what the teacher said</u>.

5 – I don't understand <u>what you just said</u>.

6 – Give me your word, I count on you.

7 – I finally recognize <u>that you were right</u>.

8 – Isabel wants to buy <u>what they have in stock</u>.

9 – Tell me <u>what you mean</u>.

10 – I know <u>what you say</u>.

Exercise E

Indicate all the noun phrase direct objects

1 – The children took all the toys in the store.

2 – For my birthday, my girlfriend will give me a brand new fax machine.

3 – Receive my sincere condolences.

4 – Give me all the pencils you took.

5 – Dr. Ross will send me a long evaluation.

6 – She does not believe you broke your watch.

7 – I think you received your grades yesterday.

8 – You and I want to buy the same used car.

Fritz-Meyer Sannon, PhD.

Exercise F

<u>Underline all the prepositional phrase objects and put a checkmark after the noun object of the preposition1 – The state gets theirs on Wednesday.</u>

2 – Campo always plays soccer after school.

3 – The students went to the library with their teachers.

4 – I put my basketball under the big chair.

5 – Ms. Rock is a nice person; she always goes to church with her new baby.

6 – Rosario does not want to go to El Salvador with Carlos.

7 – Wednesday is the fourth day of the week.

8 – Since yesterday, I have been thinking of you.

9 – Take it easy; tomorrow morning, I will be here before noon.

10 – Marie-Jose is the daughter of Mrs. Benjamin.

New English Grammar for ESL Students

Place de la Republique
Abidjan, Ivory Coast
(Africa)

Fritz-Meyer Sannon, PhD.

Chapter 13

Prepositions

Definition: A preposition (praeponere, to place before) is a particle that expresses relationship with another word such as: <u>in</u> Ecuador, <u>under</u> the table, <u>since</u> yesterday…etc.

The principal prepositions in English are:

about	despite
above	down
across	during
after	except
against	for
along	from
among	in

Fritz-Meyer Sannon, PhD.

around	inside
as	into
at	like
before	near
behind	of
below	off
beneath	on
beside	out
besides	over
between	since
beyond	through
but	throughout
by	till
to	up
toward	upon
under	with

New English Grammar for ESL Students

underneath   within

until   without

Here are some examples:

1 – I will see you **after*** the meeting.

2 – They will be **around** the house.

3 – **Before*** five o'clock, I will meet you.

4 – Mrs. Ramos went there **along** with her husband.

5 – Don't worry, the child is **behind** the door.

6 – Isabel is a quiet student, **besides** she is smart.

7 – Carmen always sits **beside** Yolanda.

8 – Xiomara puts the book **on** the teacher's desk.

9 – **Since*** yesterday, I have been sick.

10 – Everybody likes Mr. Fritz **except** Nora.

11 – She saw everything because she was looking **through** the hole.

12 – She was hiding **under** the table.

*13 – She will be here **until*** nine o'clock.*

*14 – He waited **for** his fiancée.*

*15 – Marcel left the house **without** telling me.*

Remark: Certain prepositions such as: after, before, since, etc. could be also conjunctions; as conjunctions they introduce dependent clauses usually called subordinate clauses or adverbial clauses.

Examples:

After the meetings, she left without saying a word. (**"After"** is a preposition and introduces a phrase: After the meeting)

After she left the room (**"After"** is a conjunction and introduces a clause: After she left the room.)

Before midnight, she entered her room. (**"Before"** is a preposition and introduces a phrase: Before midnight.)

Before she went to bed, she turned off the radio. (**"Before"** is a conjunction and introduces a clause: Before she went to bed…)

Since follows the same rule.

Examples: I have been in New York since 1991. (**"Since"** is a preposition and introduces a phrase: Since 1991…)

Since you are so ugly, I won't marry you. (**"Since"** is a conjunction and introduces a clause: Since you are so ugly…)

I am going to be in this room **until** seven o'clock. (**"Until"** is a preposition and introduces a phrase: Until seven o'clock.)

I will stay here until you give me your test. (**"Until"** is a conjunction and a clause: Until you give me your test…)

As we have already seen, all the subordinate conjunctions introduce subordinate, dependent of adverbial clauses.

Fritz-Meyer Sannon, PhD.

There are specific prepositions that we might use after adjectives or past participles. For instance:

Interested in

I am very interested **in** learning English.

Surprised at

I am surprised **at** his behavior; he was a very noisy student.

surrounded by

My house in Darien, Connecticut is surrounded **by** giant trees.

Angry at (a person)

The students are very angry about the noise the boys make in the hallway.

Pleased with

We are very pleased **with** the football game today.

Different from

Soccer is very different **from** the American football.

Satisfied with

The ESL students at Queens EOC are not satisfied **with** the new teacher.

Furious about

She is furious **about** the noise.

Carmen is furious **about** the weather.

Furious with

Carmen is furious **with** Yolanda.

Those boys are furious **with** that lady.

Furious for

Nora is furious **for** finishing late.

Julio is furious **for** seeing them.

Annoyed about

He is very annoyed **about** that.

Fritz-Meyer Sannon, PhD.

My mother is annoyed **about** the noise.

Annoyed with

My grandmother was annoyed **with** me.

She is annoyed **with** her classmates.

Annoyed at

She was annoyed **at** seeing them here.

Carlo is annoyed **at** getting a C-.

Jealous of (envious of; suspicious of)

I am so jealous **of** you.

I am suspicious **of** this man.

Impressed by/impressed with

I am very impressed **by** this man.

I was not very impressed **by/with** the movie.

She is very impressed **by** him.

Crazy about

I am crazy **about** classical music.

My sister is crazy **about** jazz music.

Capable/incapable of

I am capable **of** doing it alone.

She is incapable **of** driving in Manhattan.

Sorry about/for

I am sorry **about** the noise this morning.

Berta is sorry **about** her behavior.

She is sorry **about** throwing his toys in the garbage can.

Responsible for

She is responsible **for** the fire.

Alain is responsible **for** that.

Crowded with

The classroom is crowded **with** Colombians.

The street is crowded **with** cars.

Fritz-Meyer Sannon, PhD.

Tired of

The doctor is tired **of** telling his patients not to eat candies and ice cream.

Sorry for

I feel sorry **for** my wife; sometimes, she is tired out because she has to cook, clean, iron and go shopping.

There are also in English a lot of verbs which are always followed by prepositions. They can be translated by one verb in Spanish or in French. They are called idioms or two-word verbs. *Examples:*

English	*Spanish*	*French*
ask for	*pedir, preguntar*	*demander*
look for	*buscar*	*chercher*
pay for	*pagar*	*payer*
wait for	*esperar*	*attendre*
turn on	*encender, poner*	*allumer, ouvrir*

turn off	apagar, cerrar	eteindre, fermer
look at	mirar	regarder
listen to	escuchar	ecouter
put on	ponerse	mettre
take off	quitarse	enlever

Examples:

1 – The teacher **looks for** a piece of chalk.

Juan **looks for** his English book.

2 – Please **wait for** me after class.

Mercedes **waits for** her husband.

3 – **Turn off** the radio before you leave.

I want you **to turn off** the T.V.

4 – When the instructor speaks, you have to **listen to** him.

5 – **Listen to** your mother when she talks to you.

6 – **Take off** your jacket, it is so warm.

Fritz-Meyer Sannon, PhD.

My feet hurt; I want to **take off** my shoes.

However when verbs follow prepositions, it is imperative to use gerund (**ing** form). Please memorize these verbs and use them in your everyday conversation.

Examples:

*1 – I insist **on giving** him an assignment.*

*She **insisted on paying** him on time.*

*2 – We succeeded **in making** our point of view.*

*My mother has **succeeded in forcing** him to go.*

*3 – She is interested **in learning** English.*

*Marina is interested **in coming** to school.*

*4 – I am thinking **of giving** a quiz soon.*

My friend is thinking **of returning** to Cojutepeque.

Exercises

Exercise A

Underline the prepositions

1 – Before midnight, I will call you up.

2 – She insisted on giving her the form.

3 – She doesn't like to talk about school.

4 – My brother doesn't know anything about computers.

5 – Before she came, she called me up.

6 – I want to write a letter to the staff of International University.

7 – Until you give a firm commitment, I will give you the key.

8 – Dr. Ross is a very nice person, she cares about the students.

9 – Since she never opens a book, she will fail the test.

10 – This room is completely different from that one.

11 – He has been working here since November 1999.

12 – He arrived in California at 8:30 last night.

13 – After the game, he went directly home.

14 – She sits beside Carmen.

15 – Besides the fancy car she has two motocycles.

16 – I will be waiting for you until 8 o'clock.

17 – I completely disagree with the neighbor.

18 – The adverbial clause depends on the main clause.

19 – Everyday I think of you.

20 – After he came in, he took off his jacket.

Exercise B

Use each of the following prepositions in a short sentence

Ex. I will drive to Brooklyn after the rain.

1 – (after)

2 – (before)

3 – (beyond)

4 – (between)

5 – (despite)

6 – (like)

7 – (on)

8 – (over)

9 – (since)

10 – (with)

11 – (within)

12 – (without)

Exercise C

Use the correct preposition in the spaces provided

1 – Rosa is very tired ……………………..hearing the same song.

2 – Kim is very interested ………………………learning.

3 – Yolanda is never absent ………………………class.

4 – Fritz is fond ……………………classical music.

5 – My cup is filled ……………………Bustelo coffee.

6 – I know you were very please …………………….the movie.

7 – Are you please …………………………..the new teacher?

8 – The cars in the garage are covered ……………………..snow.

9 – She is sorry …………………….him.

10 – The soldiers in Afghanistan were surrounded ………………horses.

11 – Believe it or not the players are satisfied ………………the training.

12 – Do you think that Fritz is angry …………………..the students.

13 – I am sure you are not angry ………………………..me.

14 – Campo is afraid …………………….rats.

15 – My study room is full ………………………….dirty papers.

Fritz-Meyer Sannon, PhD.

New English Grammar for ESL Students

Kabul, Afghanistan
(before the war 2001)

Fritz-Meyer Sannon, PhD.

Chapter 14

Conjunctions

Definition: A conjunction is a word that joins or connects words, phrases, or clauses, sometimes sentences. There are different kinds of conjunctions:

a) Coordinate or coordinating conjunctions.

b) Correlative conjunctions.

c) Subordinate or subordinating conjunctions.

A. Coordinate or coordinating conjunctions

A coordinate or coordinating conjunction is a word that connects two words or clauses of the same nature, or same grammatical rank. The coordinating conjunctions are: *"and," "or," "but," "for," "nor," "so," "yet," "whereas."*

Fritz-Meyer Sannon, PhD.

Examples:

I like coffee <u>and</u> tea.

He loves red <u>and</u> blue.

John did it fast <u>and</u> well.

Do you like white wine <u>or</u> red wine?

Put it on my desk <u>or</u> on Norma's desk.

Love it <u>or</u> leave it.

My mother cooks <u>but</u>* my father cleans.

She is very poor <u>but</u> she is smart.

I eat it <u>but</u> I don't like it.

She goes there, <u>for</u>** she needs to be there.

I listen to her <u>for</u> she brings news to me.

He lifts that heavy table <u>for</u> he is strong.

I don't care he comes today <u>nor</u> would anyone miss him.

My girlfriend doesn't like it and <u>nor</u> do I.

That is not the real reason, <u>nor</u> is it very important.

My friend was late <u>so</u> the teacher forgave him.

I like him <u>so</u> I help him.

She doesn't show up <u>so</u>, I don't care.

She is very ugly <u>yet</u> very smart.

Mary is very sharp <u>yet</u> very lazy.

He was begging <u>yet</u> nobody helped.

He makes $2,000 <u>whereas</u>*** he receives $1,000.

John drives to school <u>whereas</u> he is always late.

My friend looks very sick <u>whereas</u> she is very healthy.

***But** is also a preposition meaning except.

Sometimes **for has the meaning of because, but it is never used at the beginning of a sentence.

*****Whereas** is used in formal speech.

B. Correlative conjunctions

Correlative conjunctions are pairs of words having mutual relation; usually used to form phrases, clauses of equal

Fritz-Meyer Sannon, PhD.

importance. The correlative conjunctions are: *as…as, both…and, either…or, neither…nor, not only…but also, so…as.*

Examples:

My cousin is <u>as</u> strong <u>as</u> my friend Pierre.

Paris is <u>as</u> beautiful <u>as</u> Madrid.

My friend speaks <u>as</u> well <u>as</u> my mentor.

<u>Both</u> boys <u>and</u> girls play in the park.

I like <u>both</u> cats <u>and</u> dogs.

<u>Both</u> women <u>and</u> men show up.

I will take <u>either</u> "F" <u>or</u> "E" train.

I don't mind, I drink <u>either</u> coffee <u>or</u> tea.

You can <u>either</u> drive <u>or</u> take the train.

I like <u>neither</u> whiskey <u>nor</u> vodka.

<u>Neither</u> John <u>nor</u> Alma is home.

<u>Neither</u> the trains <u>nor</u> the planes are safe.

Not only is she beautiful *but also* she is smart.

He plays not only tennis well, but also golf.

She is not only stupid but also mean.

She is not so tall as her brother.

I am not so rich as he is.

He is not so intelligent as he thinks he is.

C. Subordinate or subordinating conjunctions

Subordinate or subordinating conjunctions introduce subordinate clauses, also dependent clauses, because they depend on another clause:

(independent, main clause or principal.) The subordinating conjunctions are:

after (time)	if (condition)	so (that)(effect, purpose)
although (opposition)	in as much that (cause, effect)	the first time that (time)
as (time)	in case that (condition)	the last time (that) (time)

as long as (time)	in the event that (condition)	the next time that (time)
as soon as (time)	in order (that) (purpose) (cause, effect)	though (opposition)
because (cause, effect)	now that (cause, effect)	unless (condition)
before (time)	once (time)	until (time)
by the time (that) (time)	only if (condition)	when, whenever (time)
every time (that) (time)	provided (that) (condition)	whereas (opposition)
even if (condition)	providing (that) (condition)	whether or not (condition)
even though (opposition)	since (time, cause)	while (time, opposition)

Some examples with subordinate conjunctions:

Subordinate conjunctions of time

<u>Before</u> you leave, turn off the T.V.

He ate <u>before</u> I did.

<u>As long as</u> you have your ticket, you can go.

<u>Whenever</u> you want, show me the letter.

Subordinate conjunctions of opposition

<u>Although</u> she is ugly, I will marry her.

He is a very good father <u>whereas</u> he is a wise guy.

You have to do it, <u>even though</u> you don't like it.

<u>Though</u> Kim doesn't speak English well, he got an "A" on the final exam.

Subordinating conjunction of condition

<u>If</u> I have money, I will buy a car.

<u>Providing that</u> you have a pass, you can get in.

<u>If</u> I were you, I would put on my coat.

<u>Unless</u> you study hard, you will pass the test.

Subordinate conjunctions of cause

<u>Because</u> you come late, the teacher <u>will</u> be mad.

I can not buy the house <u>since</u> I don't have money.

<u>In as much as</u> the two leaders were absent, the meeting was called off.

I will marry you <u>because</u> I love you.

Note: <u>Because</u> and <u>since</u> are both subordinating conjunctions of cause, but <u>since</u> as a subordinate conjunction is weaker than <u>because</u>. Likewise <u>because</u> and <u>in as much as</u> are both subordinating conjunctions of cause. <u>In as much as</u> is used in formal speech and writing. It is better to use <u>because</u> in everyday conversation.

<u>Conjunctive adverbs</u> are also called **TRANSITIONS**. They function like conjunctions because they connect two clauses or sentences. They are: *"consequently," "furthermore," "however," "moreover," "then," "therefore."*

Here are some examples with conjunctive adverbs.

a) <u>Consequently</u>

John's car stopped in the middle of the way; <u>consequently</u> he got home late.

The students didn't study. <u>Consequently</u>, they failed.

Maria never sees a doctor. <u>Consequently</u>, she is very sick and has to go to the hospital.

b) **Furthermore**

Yolanda is a very nice person. <u>Furthermore</u>, she is very interested in learning.

Mr. Fritz is a very good professor. <u>Furthermore</u>, he has a sense of humor.

He always participates in class. <u>Furthermore</u>, he is never absent.

c) **However**

Xiomara is a good student. <u>However</u> she is always late.

It is very cool outside. <u>However</u>, it is very warm inside.

Isabel is very clever. <u>However</u>, she is too quiet.

d) **Moreover**

Queens EOC is a good institution. <u>Moreover</u>, the school has a good administrative staff.

Mr. Williams is a nice person. <u>Moreover</u>, all the student like him.

Mr. David is very professional. <u>Moreover</u>, the whole staff admires and respects him.

e) <u>Then</u>

Bring your passport and Social Security #; <u>then</u> I will see you.

If you don't have your green card; <u>then</u> you are illegal.

When you finish talking to him; <u>then</u> go to the Bursar.

f) <u>Therefore</u>

Peter did not wear his helmet. Therefore he was severely injured.

Dina never prepared her assignments. Therefore she did not pass.

Julio took the red light. Therefore, he had a tragic accident.

New English Grammar for ESL Students

Exercises

Exercise A

<u>Underline all the coordinating conjunctions</u>

1 – The rich and the poor are equal at death.

2 – Which one do you like the big or the small?

3 – Eight and eight are sixteen.

4 – Nora likes to learn English, but she hates to study.

5 – I will go there by "F" train or "E" train.

6 – After my uncle left, my aunt showed up.

7 – Tell me what you eat and I'll tell you what you are.

8 – I admire her but I don't love her.

Exercise B

<u>Underline all the correlative conjunctions</u>

1 – Both girls and boys went to the stadium.

2 – Marina will take either the "F" or "E" train.

3 – Neither Carmen nor Alma is home.

4 – Both teachers and students dance at the party.

5 – Xiomara likes either coffee or tea.

6 – I like neither whiskey nor vodka.

7 – Isabel likes both cats and dogs.

8 – You can either drive or take the bus.

Exercise C

Underline once the coordinate conjunctions and underline twice the correlative conjunctions

1 – Seven and seven are fourteen.

2 – Isabel eats the food, buy she does not like it.

3 – Which one do you like, the red or the yellow?

4 – She is as beautiful as her sister.

5 – Both men and women love pets.

6 – Jose likes neither apple cider nor rum.

7 – I like black coffee but I don't like "café au lait."

8 – I live in Brooklyn and I go to school in Queens.

Exercise D

Underline all the subordinate conjunctions

1 – Because you are smart, I will give you the job.

2 – As long as you have a valid passport, you can go home.

3 – I will pay you because you did a good job.

4 – Unless you study hard, you will not pass the test.

5 – Providing that you have a pass, you can get in.

6 – If you come on time, I will talk to you.

7 – Whenever you want, you can leave.

8 – Before you leave, turn off the light.

Exercise E

Write (SCC) after the subordinate conjunctions of cause

1 – Since I don't have money, I can't go.

2 – Today is my birthday; tomorrow will be Yolanda's birthday.

3 – My mother went to the hospital because she is sick.

4 – I go to bed because I am tired out.

5 – Before you go, get me a glass of water.

6 – Though Kim is absent from class, we celebrate her birthday.

7 – If I were you, I wouldn't go outside.

8 – Because you come late, the teacher will be mad.

Exercise F

Write (SC) after all subordinate conjunction of time

1 – I win because I always play.

2 – Don't do it to me when you come over.

3 – As long as you behave, I will welcome you.

4 – Before you go, turn off the T.V.

5 – After you pay off the whole thing, you will get a receipt.

6 – Whenever you decide I will return it to you.

7 – If you go, call me right away.

8 – When you go, say "hello" to mom.

Exercise G

Underline all the conjunctive adverbs

1 – She respects her father; <u>furthermore</u>, she loves him.

2 – If you come, you will get it; if you don't you won't get anything.

3 – Julio spends his time playing dominoes and never studies.

4 – Dina never prepares her assignments.

5 – Pedro did not wear his helmet; <u>therefore</u>, he was severely injured.

6 – Isabel is never absent; <u>however</u>, she is very shy in class.

7 – When I finish my project; <u>then</u>, I will get my degree.

8 – Marina studies hard; <u>furthermore</u>, she loves the school.

Exercise H

Write (CA) after the conjunctive adverbs and (SC) after the subordinate conjunctions.

1 – Maria never goes for a check-up, consequently she is very sick.

2 – Yolanda is a great student; furthermore she is never absent.

3 – Although I am older than you are, I know you like me.

4 – Because she is very sick, she is still in the hospital.

5 – Xiomara is an excellent student; however she is always late.

6 – Xiomara is always late, because she works far from the school.

7 – Mr.Williams is a nice person. Moreover, all the students like him.

10 – Those students did not study at all; consequently, they failed.

Fritz-Meyer Sannon, PhD.

New English Grammar for ESL Students

The house of Christopher Columbus
(Dominican Republic)

Fritz-Meyer Sannon, PhD.

Chapter 15

Interjections

Definition: Interjections are words or phrases usually used to express pleasure, sudden surprises, annoyances. Sometimes, they are formed by common words; sometimes simply by sounds.

1 – Oh!

2 – Damn!

3 – Hurray!

4 – Gosh!

5 – Hey!

6 – Wow!

etc.

1 – **Oh!** This is really sad.

Fritz-Meyer Sannon, PhD.

2 – **Damn it!** That stupid guy!

3 – **Hurray!** What is that?

4 – **Gosh!** I forget what I was going to say.

5 – **Hey!** I don't buy it.

6 – **Wow!** This is wonderful.

As we can notice the word *"interjection"* means *"throwing away", "throwing in",* meaning that most of the time interjections can stand alone; and sometimes they do not constitute a part of speech or grammatical structure. For example, adverbs of affirmation or negation are interjections on the emotion on the part of the speaker.

1 – Oh yes!

2 – Oh no!

3 – Hello!

4 – Goodbye!

1 – Oh yes, I understand very well.

2 – *Oh no, I don't accept that.*

3 – *Hello! Where are you?*

4 – *Goodbye, see you soon.*

Sometimes, interjections are not integrated in the grammatical settings. They look like strangers within the sentence structure.

1 – Oh yes, I think so.

2 – Oh no, are you crazy?

There is no relation between "oh yes" and "I think so."

There is no relation between "oh no" and "are you crazy?"

It is very important to use a comma after the interjection even though, there is no relation between what so called interjection and the rest of the sentence.

Examples:

1 – *Hello, how are you today?*

2 – *Hey, baby you are so beautiful.*

Fritz-Meyer Sannon, PhD.

3 – *Oh no, you will not get anything.*

However, if the interjection is included within the sentence, it is necessary to use two commas:

1 – I have been waiting, alas, for so long.

2 – Did you see that, John, that bum over there.

3 – Could you, damn it, do it quick.

4 – This is, my gosh, a very nice day.

5 – Look at that, wow, it's so nice.

As you have seen in #2, interjections are very complicated. Anything (a sound, a name of a person) could be used as interjections. It depends on the emotion on the part of the speaker.

The adverbs yes and no are frequently used as interjections:

1 – *Yes*, I see that.

2 – *No*, leave me alone.

3 – *Yes*, take it.

4 – *No*, I don't believe it.

5 – *Yes,* I will go with you.

Any term of direct address, any other part of speech, any sound could be used as an interjection.

Exercises

Exercise A

Underline the interjections in the following sentences

1 – Gosh! I forget it.

2 – Goodbye, sweetheart.

3 – See you soon.

4 – Wow! It's wonderful.

5 – Give me that thing at last.

6 – Oh yes, I do love it.

7 – Oh no, I don't like it at all.

8 – Hello, I am excited to meet you.

9 – Oh, I love it very much.

Exercise B

Eliminate or cross out the interjections where they are not necessary

1 – Don't give me that, John.

2 – Alas, they are not going to come today.

3 – Damn it, this boy does not understand anything.

4 – Give me some white paper, hello.

5 – I, yes, do not know his name.

6 – Wow! This is wonderful!

7 – Oh yes, I love it a lot.

8 – This is too big, wow.

9 – The children go to school, no.

Exercise C

Put the interjection words where they belong

1 – Susan, go and see, fast.

2 – See you guys, I love you.

3 – I don't know that, oh no.

4 – Oh yes, I don't believe it.

5 – Good day my friend, hello.

6 – How are you, hello.

7 – It is wonderful, wow!

8 – Alas, this is another hot day.

9 – See you tomorrow, hello.

Exercise D

<u>Use the right punctuation signs where necessary</u>

1 – Oh yes buy it if you like it.

2 – Oh no stop.

3 – White flowers white flowers I am tired of it.

4 – Honey why did you do that?

5 – Alas another hot day.

6 – Wow that is delicious.

7 – Hello my son please do it quick.

8 – Oh no darling don't go there alone.

Fritz-Meyer Sannon, PhD.

New English Grammar for ESL Students

National Theater in San Salvador
El Salvador

Fritz-Meyer Sannon, PhD.

Chapter 16

Punctuation

Definition: Punctuation is the division of phrases, clauses, and sentences by means of marks called punctuation marks (comma, semicolon, colon, period, etc.) to indicate the structure of sentence elements.

The signs of punctuation are:

Comma, period, colon, semicolon, dash, hyphen, apostrophe, parentheses, brackets, quotations, quotation marks, ellipses marks, slash.

A. <u>Comma</u> We usually use a comma before one of the following coordinating conjunctions (*and, or, but, nor, for, so, yet*) when the conjunction connects two or more words groups, or independent clauses.

Fritz-Meyer Sannon, PhD.

We commonly use a comma to name or indicate a series.

For instance:

a series with "and"
He likes football, basketball, volleyball, and golf, soccer, and ping-pong, and tennis.

a series with "or"
Although he doesn't drink alcohol, he loves to drink coffee or tea, green or herb tea.

a series of phrases
They like to go to school in the morning, and in afternoon.

a series of adjectives
Isabel is smart, she is intelligent, and she is humble.

Note: When the clauses are short, the comma is omitted.

Examples: The teacher left and we stay. It is not necessary to use a "comma" to separate word groups that are not independent clauses.

John goes home and sees his grandfather.

We also use a comma to introduce a clause especially a subordinate clause or adverb clause. *Examples:*

a) *Before you leave, turn off the television*

b) *When you come in, turn on the light in my bedroom.*

c) *Although you are poor, I love you.*

However, when the main clause introduces the sentence, it is not necessary to use a comma.

a) Turn off the television before you leave.

b) Turn on the light in my bedroom when you come in.

c) I love you although you are poor.

Finally we use a "comma" when we deal with <u>adjective clauses</u>.

What is an adjective clause? First, what is an adjective? An adjective is a word that modifies or describes a noun or pronoun. An adjective clause plays the role of a simple adjective meaning the adjective clause modifies or describes a noun or pronoun.

Fritz-Meyer Sannon, PhD.

Example:

The little boy, who is there, is my friend.

Who is there is an adjective clause. Who is there describes the little boy. Note that an adjective clause begins with a relative pronoun such as *"who," "whom," "whose," "which," "that,"* or a relative pronoun such as *"where"* or *"when."*

    a) An adjective clause could be non-restrictive or restrictive.

Non-restrictive clauses contain *"commas"* whereas restrictive clauses do not contain *"commas."*

Examples:

a) *The old house, <u>which is 100 years old</u>, is mine.*

b) *The new car, <u>which is on the other street</u>, belongs to my elder brother.*

<u>Which is 100 years old</u> is an adjective clause describing the old house.

<u>Which is on the other street</u> is another adjective clause describing the new car.

Both adjective clauses are non-restrictive clauses which are set off with commas. In reality, "which is on the other street" is not very important, is not essential; this part of the sentence could be omitted. The new car belongs to my elder brother. Also, the sentence will be OK without "which is 100 years old."

However in the restrictive sentence, the "comma" is not important.

Example: The boy <u>who wears a blue shirt</u>, is Chinese. No comma is necessary. The adjective clause who wears a blue shirt is essential, is important.

Other examples:

1) The books, <u>which are on the table</u>, are mine.

2) The books <u>that are on the table</u> are mine.

In sentence one, there is a non-restrictive clause. The commas are used; but the adjective clause is not important and can be omitted. In sentence two, there is a restrictive clause. The commas are omitted but the adjective clause is very important and cannot be omitted.

Note that a lot of grammarians prefer to use the relative pronoun "which" in non-restricted clauses, and "that" in restrictive clauses.

B. <u>Semicolon</u> is a punctuation mark [;] that usually separates coordinate clauses before a conjunctive adverb (However, therefore, etc.) The semicolon could be used like a "comma," period, or colon depending on the context.

The semicolon is frequently used between independent clauses. In this case, it precedes transitional expression that is a conjunctive adverb or a transitional phrase.

The conjunctive adverbs are	The transitional phrases are:
also	as a matter of fact
anyway	as a result
besides	at the same time
consequently	for example
finally	for instance
furthermore	in addition
however	in fact
indeed	in other words
instead	on the contrary
likewise	on the other hand
moreover	etc.
nevertheless	

Fritz-Meyer Sannon, PhD.

otherwise

still

then

therefore

etc.

Note that a "comma" always follows the transitional expression.

Examples:

1) She has not studied for a long time; therefore, she will fail the test.

2) She was very late; consequently, she missed the plane.

3) We were so tired after the training; as a matter of fact, we went to bed when we got home.

Her name isn't Mrs. White.

The class of '02 . This sounds like a song of ('60 generation)

G. <u>Period</u> 1) Periods are called "end punctuations"; they are used to end sentences except for exclamations and direct questions.

New York State Dept. of Social Services Audit and Quality Control is located in Albany, NY.

I used to work for INS.

2) A period is used in abbreviations.

Mrs. Dr. TX. NY.

Ph.D B.A. CA. NJ.

etc. M.A. CT. USA.

H. <u>Parentheses:</u> We use parentheses to enclose non essential information, minor digressions. Parentheses are also used to enclose numbers or letters.

1) There is a big difference between see and sea (see page 13).

I don't like Stamford (I mean the town in Connecticut).

From Queens to Brooklyn you can: (1) Take the BQE Highway. (2) Take Flushing train on Times Square. (3) Take #2 to Brooklyn.

Remark. Do not overuse parentheses.

I. Brackets: Brackets are usually used inside of quoted matter.

For instance:

He said that

"His son was born in 1991 [?] in a small town in California."

He declared to the judge that:

"He came in this country sometime in 1968 [?]."

The author of "Les Misérables" [Victor Hugo] was born in Besançon.

4) My brother works twelve hours a day; in addition, he goes to school every evening.

Sometimes the conjunctive adverb is in the middle or at the end of the second clause, we use the semicolon between the clauses.

Example: A lot of employees go to the cafeteria to eat and play cards; H. Bellevue, however, stays in the office on his break to read the newspaper.

Avoid semicolons between a subordinate clause and a main clause.

Examples:

Since today is a nice day; I will go to the park. (incorrect)

Since today is a nice day, I will go to the park. (correct)

Fritz-Meyer Sannon, PhD.

Avoid semicolons between an appositive and the main subject, or the word it refers to.

Example: The commander in chief of the expeditionary forces; the general Leclerc, was Napoleon Bonaparte's brother-in-law. (incorrect)

Do not use "semicolons" either between independent clauses formed by coordinating conjunctions.

1) Most of the Queens EOC teachers are very nice; and very responsible people. (incorrect)

Most of the Queens EOC teachers are very nice, and very responsible people. (correct)

2) One of the students in my ESL class is very, very intelligent; buy she talks too much. (incorrect)

One of the students in my ESL class is very, very intelligent, but she talks too much. (correct)

C. Colon [:] introduces a quotation, an explanation, an enumeration. A colon follows the salutation of a letter and separates the parts of numerical expressions. They say that colons are used to call attention to the words that follow them.

1) Colon is used after the independent clause to direct attention to a list.

Example:

a) A healthy person should avoid the following things: alcohol, cigarette, fat, etc...

b) A good ESL student needs the following: a good textbook, a good English dictionary, a good bilingual dictionary to be used at home.

We can use "colons" to direct attention to a quotation.

Ex. The American writer, Mark Twain said: "Age is a matter of mind; if you don't mind it doesn't matter."

Fritz-Meyer Sannon, PhD.

2) A colon is used between two independent clauses, when the second clause is an explanation of the first.

Example: Knowledge is power: it gives the ability, and the capacity to exercise control.

3) A colon is used after the salutation of a business letter.

Example: Dear Dr. D. Gordon: To whom it may concern...

4) A colon is finally used to distinguish hours from minutes or chapters from verses in a biblical citation.

Examples: 8h:50m   12h:40m

Jean 4:5   Paul 3:6   Genesis 12:2

D. <u>Dash</u>: Typists usually use two hyphens to form a dash (–); the function of a dash is to emphasize:

1) Sometimes, the dash shows a change of thought.

Example: The instructors at the State University of New York – of course, I do not mean you – are very nice.

2) We use a dash for a listing of what is stated in the sentence, for a reinstatement, or for a shift in thought.

Example: Come to school on time, be prepared for the assignment, participate in class – all of those are important to be a good student.

E. **Hyphen** 1) **A hyphen is used to make a compound word out of two or three words (to become one).**

Examples :   Fritz-Meyer,   Jean-Paul,   Jean-Robert, Jean-Pierre

I like to see her in that blue-green blouse.

2) Hyphen is also used when a word is broken at the end of the line because of lack of space.

Examples:

Amb-

itious

negli-

Fritz-Meyer Sannon, PhD.

gent

3) The hyphen is used in compound numbers; it is used to separate date of birth and date of death.

Examples: Joseph: 1917-1953

George Harrison: 1943-2001

F. <u>Apostrophe</u> 1) Apostrophe is used to show possession, possessive case of nouns.

The student's car.

The employee's briefcase.

or the instructor's desk. Etc.

2) The apostrophe is used to show plurals of nouns. If, for instance, the noun is plural and ends in "s" we add an apostrophe:

The students' car.

The boys' toys.

3) Use apostrophe to show omissions in contractions and numbers.

We don't know where Donna is.

The existentialist woman, author of the "Second Sex" [Simone de Beauvoir] didn't die in the U.S.A.

J. Quotations: We use quotations or quotation marks to indicate titles or short works, titles of chapters, essays etc.

"The Taliban's background" (short works)

"The first rooms" (title of chapter)

"The boy's school" (essays)

"The bad girls" (one act play)

Fritz-Meyer Sannon, PhD.

New English Grammar for ESL Students

Do you like squirrels?
Really?

Fritz-Meyer Sannon, PhD.

Appendix A

Euphemisms

Definition: Euphemism is a substitution of a mild expression for one that might offend somebody; it is also an expression that is gentler than the one usually used that sounds unpleasant.

Examples: Pass away for die.

Senior citizen for old

Washroom for toilet.

Here is a listing of the most common euphemisms:

1 – Charlie Brown   Pie

2 – Adult Entertainment   Pornography

3 – Archivist   Library clerk

4 – Bloody (British)   Damn (sh**)

Fritz-Meyer Sannon, PhD.

5 – Bulrush		Illegitimate child
6 – Crowd Engineer		Police dog
7 – Creative conflict		Civil rights demonstration
8 – Cardiovascular Accident		Stroke
9 – Bite the Dust		Die
10 – Casket		Coffin
11 – Chemical Dependency		Drug addiction
12 – Correctional Facility		Prison
13 – Economically Deprived		Poor
14 – Expecting		Pregnant
15 – Exceptional Child		Retarded child
16 – Expectorate		Spit
17 – Finalize		End
18 – Feeling no pain		Drunk
19 – Food preparation center		Kitchen
20 – Give early retirement		Dismiss

21 – First joint   Leg (chicken food)

22 – Hairk   Hair cut

23 – Kick the bucket   Dead

24 – Billy Ryan   Goatee

25 – Intoxicated   Drunk

26 – In trouble   Pregnant

27 – In the buff   Naked

28 – In the family way   Pregnant

29 – In the sunset years Old

30 – In the twilight years Old

31 – John   Toilet

32 – Lung affliction   Tuberculosis

33 – Love child   Illegitimate child

34 – Make love   Sexual intercourse

35 – Mistress   Kept woman

36 – Make out   Kissing

37 – Memorial park	Cemetery
38 – Moisture	Sweat
39 – Not renew the contract	Dismiss
40 – Negative savings	Debts
41 – Nuclear engagement	Nuclear war
42 – One over the eight	Drunk
43 – Powder one's nose	Go to the toilet
44 – Legless	Drunk
45 – Log lifter	Really heavy rain
46 – Meet one's end	Die
47 – Make away with oneself	Suicide
48 – Pay the supreme sacrifice	To be dead
49 – Pass away	Die
50 – Pop off	To be dead
51 – Plastered	Drunk
52 – Opportunity school	School for retarded

53 – Park under construction   Town Dump

54 – Obsequies   Funeral

55 – Of advanced years   Old

56 – Perspire   Sweat

57 – Optically challenged   Blind

58 – Powder room   Toilet

59 – Problem skin   Acne

60 – The plumbing   Toilet

61 – Pre-owned automobile   Used car

62 – Prevaricate   Lie

63 – Prevaricator   Liar

64 – Plant food   Manure, Fertilizer

65 – The little boy's room   Toilet

66 – Rotund   Fat

67 – Roll in the hay   Sexual intercourse

68 – So many years young   Old

Fritz-Meyer Sannon, PhD.

69 – Separate from payroll　　　Fire

70 – Separate from School　　　Expel

71 – Scent　　　Smell

72 – Senior citizen　　　Old person

73 – Rest in peace　　　Die, to be dead

74 – Revenue enhancers　　　Taxes

75 – Sanitary engineer　　　Garbage collector

76 – The smallest room　　　Toilet

77 – Rooster　　　Cockerel

78 – Selected out　　　Fired

79 – Stomach　　　Belly

80 – Slow learner　　　Unintelligent learner

81 – Strategic withdrawal　　　Retreat, defeat

82 – Social disease　　　Syphilis

83 – Tired and emotional　　　Drunk

84 – Trial marriage　　　Free love

New English Grammar for ESL Students

85 – Tissue					Toilet paper

86 – Smallch					Small change

87 – Underprivileged			Poor

88 – Shovel tooth				Doctor

89 – Spend a penny			Go to the toilet

90 – Take a slask				Go to the toilet

91 – Three sheets to the wind		Drunk

92 – Trash lifter				Heavy rain

93 – Uniquely abled			Physically disabled

94 – Tidily					Drunk

95 – Top oneself				Suicide

96 – Wash one's hand			Go to the toilet

97 – Wearing only a smile		Naked

98 – Wash room				Toilet

99 – White meat				Thigh (chicken)

100 – Without a stitch			Naked

Fritz-Meyer Sannon, PhD.

New English Grammar for ESL Students

These are raccoons.
They are beautiful.

Fritz-Meyer Sannon, PhD.

Appendix B

Listing of 200 troublesome words in American English

1 – <u>Abjure</u>: (v) to renounce upon oath.

2 - <u>Adjure</u>: (v) to request somebody solemnly to do something.

3 – <u>Accidently</u>: meaning by accident (unacceptable)

4 - <u>Accidentally</u>: (adv) meaning by chance, often mispronounced, misspelled.

5 - <u>Adherence</u>: (n) firm attachment. Act of adhering.

6 -<u>Adherents</u>: (n) follower, supporter, adherent. (adj)

7 – <u>Adopted</u>: (adj & verb, (to choose) one taken by other legally.

8 – <u>Adopted</u>: (adj) made by adoption.

9 – <u>Adverse</u>: (adj) acting against (refers to opinion, intention)

10 – <u>Averse</u>: (adj) reluctant, having an aversion. (feeling, inclination)

11 – <u>Advice</u>: (n) recommendation regarding a decision. *Example: Give an advice to someone.*

12 – <u>Advise</u>: (v) to give advice. *Example: I advise you to study.*

13 – <u>Afterward</u>: (adv) at a later time. Mostly used in USA.

14 – <u>Afterwards</u>: (adv) at a later time. Mostly used in England.

15 – <u>Aisle</u>: (n) corridor, a passage, row of seats in a hall.

16 – <u>Isle</u>: (n) Island, a small island. (poetic)

17 – <u>I'll</u>: contraction of "I will" or "I shall."

18 – <u>All ready</u>: (adj) completely ready; we are all ready.

19 – <u>Already</u>: previously. *Example: We have already painted the house.*

20 – <u>All together</u>: Together. Everybody in one place.

21 – <u>Altogether</u>: (adv) wholly, on the whole.

22 – <u>Assistance</u>: (n) support, help.

23 – <u>Assistants</u>: (n) people who assist, helpers.

24 – <u>Aural</u>: relates to the ear or the sense of hearing.

25 – <u>Oral</u>: spoken, not written.

26 – <u>Avert</u>: (v) to turn away, to prevent.

27 – <u>Divert</u>: to go different ways. To amuse, to entertain.

28 – <u>Award</u>: (n) a judgment, decision. Verb = to give a prize. To observe.

29 – <u>Reward</u>: compensation for services. *Something given in return for good or evil.*

30 – <u>Bale</u>: (n) a large bundle of goods. *As a verb: to make up into bales.*

31 – <u>Bail</u>: (n) security for appearance of a prisoner. *As a verb: to release under bail.*

32 – <u>Begin</u>: to start, to originate. *The game will begin in one hour.*

33 – <u>Commence</u>: is stronger and more formal than begin. (Law)

34 – <u>Beside</u>: (prep) meaning next to.

35 – <u>Besides</u>: (prep) meaning except; as an adverb: means in addition to.

36 – <u>Big</u>: refers to generosity, kindness. *A big lady, a big show.*

37 – <u>Large</u>: refers to size, immensity; more important than big.

38 – <u>Blue</u>: (adj) refers to color.

39 – <u>Blew</u>: (v) past tense of the verb to blow.

40 – <u>Bloc</u>: means a group. *Example: A bloc of congressmen.*

41 – Block: refers to a neighborhood, town. *Block association.*

42 – Break: (v) to fracture, to separate suddenly into parts.

43 – Brake: (n) any device for slowing up or stopping motion. (v) to slow up by a brake.

44 – Capital: goods, important city. Anything is used to increase one's power or influence.

45 – Capitol: an edifice, a building in which a state legislature meets.

46 – Complement: anything to complete. As a verb: to complete.

47 – Compliment: an expression of admiration.

48 – Core: central part of anything, especially of fruit.

49 – Corps: group of persons organized under same direction.

50 – <u>Dear</u>: beloved, expensive. Affectionately. At high price.

51 – <u>Deer</u>: animal distinguished by the solid branching horns (Red deer, Europe; Virginia deer, East USA.)

52 – <u>Device</u>: *plan, difference, invention.* Something designed to bring about a desired result.

53 – <u>Devise</u>: to invent, to will, to distribute.

54 – <u>Die</u>: to become extinct, to cease to live.

55 – <u>Dye</u>: color produced by dyeing, to stain, to color.

56 – <u>Discrete</u>: separate, individually distinct.

57 – <u>Discreet</u>: prudent, having or showing good judgment.

58 – <u>Disinterested</u>: not influenced by one's own interest, impartial.

59 – <u>Uninterested</u>: not interested.

60 – <u>Dual</u>: of two; system found on a double principle. *The dual number.*

61 – <u>Duel</u>: a combat between two persons, two opponents fought with deadly weapons.

62 – <u>Elicit</u>: to bring about, to draw. *The judge tried to elicit the truth from the defendant.*

63 – <u>Illicit</u>: illegal, not permitted, improper.

64 – <u>Licit</u>: opposite of illicit.

65 – <u>Ensure</u>: to make certain.

66 – <u>Insure</u>: to take necessary measure.

67 – <u>Every one</u>: refers to each person of a group.

68 – <u>Everyone</u>: everybody (everyone is considered as more elegant, more formal.)

69 – <u>Example</u>: pattern, model, specimen; part of something.

70 – <u>Instance</u>: example that can be illustrated.

71 – <u>Exist</u>: to have life, to live.

72 – <u>Subsist</u>: to have life.

73 – <u>Exotic</u>: strange, exciting, foreign origin, not native.

74 – <u>Esoteric</u>: secret, understood by chosen few; abstruse.

75 – <u>Expand</u>: to open wide; to enlarge.

76 – <u>Expend</u>: to consume, to use up, to spend.

77 – <u>Explicit</u>: clear, distinctly stated.

78 – <u>Implicit</u>: fairly hard to be understood, not directly stated; implied.

79 – <u>Fair</u>: impartial, pleasing to the eye. Clean, just; evenly.

80 – <u>Fare</u>: price, charge for transporting people.

81 – <u>Faze</u>: (fease or feaze) to bother, to disturb.

82 – <u>Phase</u>: any aspect or side, as of a situation or question. A temporary condition.

83 – <u>Feat</u>: neat, skillful. Courageous act, exploit.

84 – <u>Feet</u>: plural of foot.

85 – <u>Final</u>: (adj) the end; last, conclusive.

86 – <u>Finale</u>: (n) close, ending, the concluding part of an event.

87 – <u>Find</u>: to meet with, to provide, to perceive, to arrive at.

88 – <u>Fine</u>: finished, refined, end, money exacted as a penalty for an offense.

89 – <u>Forward</u>: in front, located, located in advance.

90 – <u>Foreword</u>: preface, introduction. *The foreword of the book.*

91 – <u>Froward</u>: disobedient; unwilling to do what is right.

92 – <u>Halve</u>: to divide into equal parts.

93 – <u>Have</u>: to possess, to own; as auxiliary verb: indicating completed action.

94 – <u>Hay</u>: dry grass or other plants.

95 – <u>Hey</u>: to call attention or express surprise.

96 – <u>Healthful</u>: health giving; healthful environment.

97 – <u>Healthy</u>: in a state of health.

98 – <u>Holy</u>: spiritually perfect; sacred.

99 – <u>Wholly</u>: entirely; completely.

100 – <u>Homonyms</u>: word like another in spelling or sound, but different in meaning.

101 – <u>Homograph</u>: word same spelling with another, different meaning.

102 – <u>Homophone</u>: word pronounced the same as another, same sound, sometimes same spelling, but different meaning.

103 – <u>Hours</u>: (n) sixty minutes. *Example: In two hours there are 120 minutes.*

104 – <u>Ours</u>: possessive pronoun (*mine, yours, his, hers, ours, theirs*)

105 – <u>Hypercritical</u>: too, excessively exact.

106 – <u>Hypocritical</u>: a person who pretends falsely to be better than he is. Hypocrite.

107 – <u>Idle</u>: lazy, unemployed.

108 – <u>Idol</u>: false god.

109 – <u>Idyll</u>: or idyl romantic poem.

110 – <u>Infect</u>: to contaminate, to stain.

111 – <u>Inject</u>: to introduce a new element.

112 – <u>Infest</u>: to trouble or repeated visits. *Fleas infest dogs.*

113 – <u>Isle</u>: is a poetic form of island; little island.

114 – <u>Aisle</u>: a corridor, a narrow passage.

115 – <u>Interject</u>: to put between, to introduce between parts.

116 – <u>Interpolate</u>: same meaning but refers to written matter of material that is false.

117 – <u>Its</u>: possessive form (*mine, yours, his, hers, its, etc.*) no apostrophe.

118 – <u>It's</u>: contraction of it is.

119 – <u>Kind of</u>: (**never put an article after these expressions**)

120 – <u>Sort of</u>: (don't say *this kind of a car…)

121 – <u>Knew</u>: past tense of the verb know.

122 – <u>New</u>: (adjective)

123 – <u>Knight</u>: a military attendant devoted to the service of a lady. *In modern times, a man on whom an honor has been conferred by a sovereign.* The honor is not hereditary.

124 – <u>Night</u>: the opposite of day.

125 – <u>Knot</u>: a tie, a bow. A unit of speed, equivalent to one nautical mile (6,080.20 feet) an hour; as a verb, it means to tie, to unite closely.

<u>Not</u>: an adverbial participle of negation.

126 – <u>Leave</u>: to go away, depart from.

127 – <u>Let</u>: to permit, to allow, to lease, to rent.

128 – <u>Lend</u>: to allow the use of, on condition.

129 – <u>Loan</u>: a sum of money lent at interest.

130 – <u>Borrow</u>: to receive with the intention of return. Opposite of lend.

131 – <u>Lessee</u>: a tenant under a lease.

132 – <u>Lessor</u>: one who leases. (Law)

133 – <u>Lessen</u>: to shrink, to make less.

134 – <u>Lesson</u>: something to learn or to study. Instruction.

135 – <u>Liable</u>: responsible, obligated by law.

136 – <u>Libel</u>: defamation by written or printed words, pictures, etc.

177 – <u>Lunch</u>: light meal eaten between breakfast and dinner.

138 – <u>Luncheon</u>: in a special occasion, a formal occurrence, use luncheon.

139 – <u>Lyric</u>: is used more often, is applied to poetry with musical quality.

140 – <u>Lyrical</u>: same as above. *Example: Lyric or lyrical love letters.*

141 – <u>Magic</u>: anything that produces results through mysterious influences.

142– <u>Magical</u>: same as above. Less used.

143– <u>Maid</u>: a young unmarried woman; a female servant.

144 – <u>Made</u>: part tense of make; manufactured.

145 – <u>Marshal</u>: any of various officers whose duties such as those of a sheriff; in some cities head of the Police Dept. Also leader of a parade.

146 – <u>Marshall</u>: common last name of people.

147 – <u>Misogamy</u>: hatred of marriage.

148 – <u>Misogyny</u>: hatred of women.

149 – <u>Mode</u>: fashion, mood, and arrangement.

150 – <u>Mowed</u>: past tense of mow, to cut down grass with a machine.

151 – <u>Moral</u>: manner, customs, habit, affecting standards of conduct.

152 – <u>Morale</u>: mental condition.

153 – <u>Neuter</u>: (adj) neither masculine nor feminine.

154 – <u>Neutral</u>: (adj) not taking part on either side.

155 – <u>None</u>: not any, not one. Sometimes followed by of.

156 – <u>Nun</u>: woman belonging to a religious order.

157 – <u>Official</u>: a person in office or authority; formal approval by authority.

158 – <u>Officious</u>: volunteering services where they are neither asked nor needed.

159 – <u>Omnipotent</u>: having unlimited power.

160 – <u>Omniscient</u>: knowing everything.

161 – <u>Personal</u>: private, relating to a person.

162 – <u>Personnel</u>: the body of persons employed in private or public office.

163 – <u>Poor</u>: not efficient, not good, opposite of rich.

164 – <u>Pore</u>: a tiny opening in the skin, a leaf, etc.

165 – <u>Pour</u>: to flow, to cause to flow in a stream.

166 – <u>Principal</u>: chief, leader, highest in authority.

167 – <u>Principle</u>: fundamental truth or law, rule of conduct.

168 – <u>Real</u>: actual, having existence outside the mind.

169 – <u>Reel</u>: a small, revolvable wheel; a quantity of thread, wire etc.

170 – <u>Red</u>: (adj) any color of the spectrum lying between orange and violet.

171 – <u>Read</u>: past tense of the verb to read. (Rid)

172 – <u>Sew</u>: to unite by stitches with thread and needle.

173 – <u>So</u>: in order that, for this, for that reason, therefore, etc.

174 – <u>Sow</u>: (n) to spread, to dispense, to disseminate.

175 – <u>Signature</u>: we use signature for important documents.

176 – <u>Autograph</u>: they (celebrities) give an autograph (assumed name) to those who ask for.

177 – <u>Simile</u>: expresses resemblance directly but by using as, like, or as if.

178 – Metaphor: a figure of speech which implies likeness by speaking of one thing as if it were the other thing.

179 – Smell: is the most general, most used, could be pleasant or unpleasant.

180 – Stink: refers to disagreeable or unpleasant odors.

181 – Scent: applies to distinctive odor.

182 – Straight: (adj) direct. As an adverb: directly.

183 – Strait: restricted, a narrow passage of water.

184 – Team: number of persons associated together.

185 – Teem: to be prolific, to swarm.

186 – Tic: spasmodic (periodic) motion of the muscles of the face.

187 – Tick: a small mark, to mark with a small tick.

188 – To: (prep) in the direction of; used with the infinitive expressing intention, wish, purpose, etc.

Fritz-Meyer Sannon, PhD.

189 – <u>Two</u>: numeral cardinal adjective. *Example: Two boys and two girls.*

190 – <u>Too</u>: (adv) also; likewise; more than enough. *Example: It's too sweet for me.*

191 – <u>Undo</u>: (v) nullify. To bring to ruin. To render null.

192 – <u>Undue</u>: (v) exceeding – violating legal rights.

193 – <u>University</u>: institution of higher learning that has two or more colleges.

194 – <u>College</u>: a college or smaller awards degree for undergraduate work. Rarely offers Masters degree. Queens College.

195 – <u>Unqualified</u>: not having proper qualifications.

196 – <u>Disqualified</u>: loss of rights or privileges.

197 – <u>Vein</u>: blood vessel. Anything that runs through something else.

198 – <u>Vane</u>: (n) a device to show the way the wind blows.

199 – <u>Vain</u>: (adj) (vanus, empty, void) no real value, useless, futile.

200 – <u>Vice</u>: immoral conduct. A prefix meaning one who takes the place of. *Example: Vice-consul, vice-president.*

201 – <u>Vise</u>: (n) screw, any device for holding or clamping work.

202 – <u>Visit</u>: (v) to go to see.

203 – <u>Visit with</u>: to stay with for some time. To communicate without physical presence. *Example: I will visit with you tomorrow.*

204 – <u>Wave</u>: (v) movement of the hand from side to side. To swing back and forth.

205 – <u>Waive</u>: (v) to choose not to insist on something. I waive my right.

206 – <u>Won't</u>: is the contraction of will not. (*Negative future*)

207 – <u>Wont</u>: is a noun, is also an adjective; habit, practice, used to, accustomed.

208 – <u>Where</u>: (adv) refers to a place.

209 – <u>Wear</u>: (v) to have something on like clothes or ornaments.

210 – <u>Were</u>: (v) plural of was (*past tense of the verb to be*).

211 – <u>Ware</u>: (n) manufactured goods. Articles offered for sale.

212 – <u>Whose</u>: possessive of who. Whose umbrella is that?

213 – <u>Who's</u>: is the contraction for who is, who has.

top left: Blue eyed white Persian
top right: Russian blue
bottom left: Tailless Manx
bottom right: Burnese

Cats like people.
People like cats.

Fritz-Meyer Sannon, PhD.

New English Grammar for ESL Students

Appendix C

100 American Proverbs Translated in Spanish and French

| **English** | **Spanish** | **French** |

1. Actions speak louder than words.   Las acciones hablan más fuerte que las palabras.   Les actions parlent plus fort que les mots.

2. A friend in need is a friend indeed.   Amigo en la adversidad es amigo de verdad.   C'est dans l'adversité qu'on connait les vrais amis.

3. All that glitters is not gold.   No to lo que brilla es oro.   Tout ce qui brille n'est pas or.

4. An apple a day keeps the doctor away.   Una manzana cada día de médico te curaría.   Il vaut mieux aller au moulin qu'au médecin.

5. A bird in the hand is worth two in the bus.   Un pájaro en la mano vale dos volando.   Un tien vaut mieux que deux tu l'auras.

6. Ask and you shall receive.   El que busca encuenta.   Demande tu reçevras.

7. Barking dogs seldom bite.	Perro ladrador, poco mordedor.	Tous les chiens qui aboient ne mordent pas.
8. Beauty is in the eye of the beholder.	Quien fero ama hermoso la parece.	Il n'y a pas de laides amours.
9. Beggars can't be choosers.	Quien pide no escoge.	Nécessité fait la loi.
10. Better the day, better the deed.	Buen día, buen trabajo.	Bon jour, bonne oeuvre.
11. Better the devil you know than the devil you don't know.	Más vale malo conocido que bueno por conocer.	Il vaut mieux un danger qu'on connaît, qu'un danger qu'on ne connait pas.
12. Better safe than sorry.	Mas vale precaver que tener que lamentar.	Prévenir vaut mieux que guérir/deux précautions valent mieux qu'une.
13. Birds of a feather flock together.	Dime con quien andas y te dire quien eres.	Qui se ressemble s'assemble.
14. Blood is thicker than water.	La sangre pésa mas que el agua.	Le sang appelle le sang.
15. Charity begins at home.	La caridad bien entendida empieza por casa	Charité bien ordonnée commence par soi-même.

16. Closed mouth catches no flies.	En la boca cerrada no entran moscas.	Pas de succes sans écueil.
17. A cat may look at a king	Los ojos son para mirar con mirar no se desgasta.	Un chien regarde bien un évèque.
18. Clothes do not make the monk.	El hábito no hace al monje.	L'habit ne fait pas le moine.
19. Do as I say, not as I do	Haz tu lo que bien digo y no lo que mal hago.	Fais ce que je dis, mais pas ce que je fais.
20. Dogs don't eat dogs.	Perro no come perro.	Les loups ne se mangent pas entre eux.
21. Does the cat have your tongue? Or have you swallowed your tongue?	Te comieron la langua? o te ha comido la langua el gato?	As-tu avalé ta langue?
22. Don't burn your bridges behind you	Nadie diga: De esta agua no bebere.	Il ne faut pas dire fontaine, je ne boirai pas de ton eau.
23. Don't count your chickens before they hatch.	No cuentas les pollos antes de que salgan del cascarón.	Il ne faut pas vendre la peau de l'ours avant de l'avoir tué.
24. Don't cry over spilt milk.	No llores sobre la leche derramada.	Ce qui est fait, est fait.

25. Don't judge a book by its cover,	Las aparencias enganan.	Il ne faut pas juger les gens sur la mine.
26. Don't look a gift horse in the mouth.	Un caballo regalado no se le mira el colmillo.	A cheval donné on ne regarde pas la bride.
27. Don't put the cart before the horse.	No pongas la carreta delante de los caballos.	Il ne faut jamais mettre la charrue avant les boeufs.
28. Don't put off tomorrow what you can do today.	No dejes para mañana lo puedas hacer hoy.	Ne renvoie jamais à demain ce que tu peux faire aujourd'hui.
29. Empty vessels make the most noise.	Mucho ruido y pocas nueces.	Les tonneaux vides font plus de bruit.
30. Friendship is love without its wings.	Es bien de tener una Amistad incondicional.	L'amitié, c'est l'amour sans les ailes.
31. Good things come in small packages.	Los Buenos perfumes vienen en vases pequeños.	Dans les petites boites, les bons onguents.
32. There is snake in the grass.	Hay traidor o Judas entre nosotros.	Il y a anguille sous roche.
33. Haste makes waste.	Visteme despacio que voy deprisa.	La hate est l'ennemie de la précision.

34. Hear the other side and believe little.	Escucha la otra campana.	Qui n'entend qu'une cloche n'entend qu'un son.
35. It's raining cats and dogs.	Está lloviendo a cántaros o llueva chuzosos.	Il pleut averse ou il tombe des cordes.
36. If you lie down with dogs, you will get up with fleas.	El que anda con lobos, a aullar se enseña.	Qui se couche avec les chiens se lève avec les puces.
37. If you can't stand the heat, get out of the kitchen.	El que tiene de cera no debe pararse al sol.	Qui craint le danger ne doit pas aller en mer.
38. Imitation is the sincerest form of flattery.	La imitación es el major halago.	L'imitation est la forme la plus fidèle de la flatterie.
39. In unity there is strength.	En la unión está la fuerza.	L'unoin fait la force.
40. Know how to work the system.	Familiarízate con el systema.	Connaitre les ficelles du métier.
41. Leave well enough alone.	Más vale solo que mal acompanado.	Le mieux est l'ennemi du bien.
42. Life goes on.	La vida continúa.	Un clou chasse l'autre.

43. Like father, like son.	De tal palo, tal astilla.	Tel père, tel fils.
44. Let sleeping dogs lie.	A enemigo que hulle, puenta de plata.	Ne reveillez pas le chat qui dort.
45. Love is blind.	El amor es ciego.	L'amour est aveugle.
46. Love makes the world go around.	El amor hace girar al mundo.	L'amour fait danser le monde.
47. Make hay while the sun shines.	Rocoge el heno mientras el sol brilla.	Battre le fer quand il est chaud.
48. A man's gravy is another man's poison.	El piso de uno es el techo de otro,	Ce qui guérit l'un tue l'autre.
49. A man's home is his castle.	La case de un hombre es su castillo.	Charbonnier est maître chez lui.
50. Little things please little minds.	Es bueno de ayudarse mutualmente.	Un âne gratte l'autre.
51. The meek shall inherit the earth.	Un día la tierra pertenecerá a los sumisos.	Aux innocents, les mains pleines.
52. Might makes right.	No hay razón como la del bastón.	La raison du plus fort est toujours la meilleure.

New English Grammar for ESL Students

53. Misinfortune never comes alone.	Como el perro del hortelano, ni come, ni deja comer.	Un malheur ne vient jamais seul.
54. Money talks.	Con dinero baila el perro.	L'argent est roi.
55. No pain, no gain.	No hay atajo sin trabajo.	Il faut casser le noyau avoir l'amande. (Or) nul bien sans peine.
56. Necessity knows no law.	La necessitad es la madre de la invención.	La faim chasse le loup du bois.
57. Never say die.	Mientras hay vira hay esperanza.	Il ne faut jamais jeter le manche après la cognée.
58. Nice guys finish last.	Cría cuevos y te sacarán los ojos.	Qui se fait brebis, le loup le mange.
59. Nothing is certain than death and taxes.	Todo tiene solucion menos la muerte.	Tout a une solution, à l'exception de la mort.
60. Never say never.	No hay quederse por vencido.	Il ne faut jamais dire "fontaine, je ne boirai pas de ton eau!"
61. Opportunity makes a thief.	La occasión hace al ladrón.	L'occasion fait le larron.
62. One swallow	Una golondrima no	Une hirondelle ne fait

does not make a summer.	hace verano.	pas le printemps.
63. Once bitten, twice shy.	El gato escalado del agua fría huye.	Chat échouffé craint l'eau froide.
64. One good turn deserves another.	Amor con amor se paga.	Un petit service en vaut un autre.
65. Only the rich get richer.	El dinero se va con el dinero.	On ne prête qu'aux riches.
66. Possession is nine-tenths of the law.	El que se fue a sevilla, perdio la silla.	Possession vaut loi.
67. Practice makes perfect.	La práctica perfecciona.	C'est en forgeant qu'on devient forgeron.
68. Punctuality is the politeness of kings.	La puntualidad es un atributo de reyes.	L'exactitude est la politesse des rois.
69. The pen is mightier than the sword.	La pluma es más poderosa que la espada.	La raison du plus fort est toujours la meilleure.
70. The road to hell is full of good intentions.	El camino hasta el infierno esta lleno de buenas intenciones.	L'enfer est pavé de bonnes intentions.
71. The style is the man.	El hábito hace el monje.	Le style fait l'homme même.

72. Speak of the devil.	Hablando del Diablo	Quand on parle du loup, n en voit la queue.
73. Step out of line and you lose your place.	El que se fue a sevilla, perdó la silla.	Qui va à la chasse perd sa place.
74. The squeaking wheel gets the oil.	Niño que no llora no mama.	A bon chien, il ne vient jamais un bon os.
75. Set a thief to catch a thief.	Nada major que un ladrón para attrapar a otro ladrón.	A bon chat, bon rat.
76. Seize the moment.	Hay que vivir en el momento.	Il faut vivre dans l'instant.
77. Slow and steady wins the race.	Visteme despacio que voy de prisa	Rien ne sert de courir, il faut partir à point.
78. Step out of line and you'll lose you place.	Quien fue a sevilla perdio su silla.	Qui va à la chasse perd sa place.
79. Talkers are not doers.	El que habla mucho, hace poco.	Ce n'est pas la vache qui crie le plus fort qui donne le plus de lait.
80. That's baseball.	No es serio.	C'est la guerre.

81. Punishment doesn't always fit the crime.	Hay criminales que no Pagan por sus crímenes.	La peine n'est pas toujours proportionnée au délit.
82. There are no problems. there are solutions.	No hay problemas since solutions.	Impossible n'est pas français.
83. To each his own.	Cada persona puede ver una cosa diferentemente.	Chacun voit midi à sa porté.
84. Too many cooks spoil the broth.	Muchos maestros cohonden la novia.	Trop de cuisiniers gatent la sauce. (Or) autant de têtes autant d'avis.
85. Variety is the spice of life.	En la verdád est el gusto.	Il faut de tout pour faire un monde.
86. Walls have ears.	Las paredes oyen.	Les murs ont des oreilles.
87. A warm Christmas spells cold weather for Easter.	Si hace buen tiempo en la Navidad, no lo hara en la Pascua.	Noël au balcon, Pâques aux tisons.
88. When in Rome, do as the Romans.	A donde fueres haz lo que vieres.	A Rome, il faut vivre comme les Romains.
89. When the cat is away, the mice will play.	Cuando los gatos están amarrados, los ratones andan	Quand le chat n'est pas là les souris dancent.

play.	sueltos.	dancent.
90. Where there is a will, there is a way.	Querer es poder.	Vouloir, c'est pouvoir.
91. Where there is smoke, there is a fire.	Donde fuego se hace, humo sale.	Il n'y a pas de fumée sans feu.
92. Woman is the key of the house.	Una casa sin madre es una casa sin cauce.	La femme est la cléf de la maison.
93. What a day may bring, a day may take away.	Cada dia es diferente.	Les jours se suivent et ne se ressemblent pas.
94. What is done, is done.	A lo hecho, pecho	Ce qui est fait, est fait.
95. You can lead a horse to water but you can't make him drink.	Se puede llevar el caballo al abrevadero, pero no obligarlo a beber.	On ne peut pas forcer les gens à faire ce qu'ils ne veulent pas.
96. You can't have the cake and eat it too.	No puedas tener el pastel y comerlo al mismo tiempo.	On ne peut avoir le beurre et l'argent du beurre.
97. You can't teach old dogs new tricks.	Loro viejo no aprende a hablar.	On n'apprend pas à un vieux singe à faire des grimaces.
98. Youth is wasted on the young.	Si la juventud supuera, si la vejez	Si jeunesse savait, si vieillesse pouvait.

on the young.	pudiera.	vieillesse pouvait.
99. You catch more flies with with honey than vinagre.	Con una gota de miel que con un cuanto de vinagre.	On n'attrappe pas le mouches avec du vinaigre.
100. You give a little, you get a lot.	No esperes que te devuelran mas de lo que tu das.	Il faut savoir donner un oeuf pour avoir un boeuf.

New English Grammar for ESL Students

Me again,
Mr. Squirrel

Fritz-Meyer Sannon, PhD.

New English Grammar for ESL Students

Appendix D

200 American idioms students should know

(in alphabetical order with their meaning in Spanish and French)

	English	Spanish	French
	<u>English</u>	<u>Spanish</u>	<u>French</u>
1.	all day long	todo el día	toute la journée
2.	all of a sudden	repentinamente	tout d'un coup
3.	as a matter of fact	en realidad, es más	le fait est que
4.	as usual	como de costumbre	comme d'habitude
5.	at all	nada	du tout
6.	at last	por fin	enfin
7.	at least	por lo menos	au moins
8.	at once	inmediatamente	tout de suite
9.	at times	a veces	quelques fois

10.	back out	retirarse, decidir en contrario	changer d'avis
11.	back up	ir para atrás	conduire en arrière
12.	be better off	estar major	valoir mieux
13.	be becoming	quedarle bien	être seyant
14.	be bound for	dirigirse a	à destination de
15.	become of	suceder	advenir
16.	be cut out for	tener talento para	avoir l'étoffe de
17.	be in the way	estorbar	être de trop
18.	be named after	nombrador por	être nommé pour
19.	be out of the question	ser imposible	être impossible
20.	be up	terminado	être terminé
21.	be struck	ser enganado	être volé
22.	be used to	estar acostumbrado	être accoutumé à
23.	be well off	ser rico	dans l'aisance

24.	blow down	echar al suelo	abattre
25.	blow out	reventarse	avoir une crevaison
26.	break down	romperse	ne plus marcher
27.	break into	entrar en, as altar	s'introduire
28.	break loose	soltarse	se détacher de
29.	break off	terminar	romper avec
30.	bring about	efectuar	rapporter
31.	bring out	presentar	présenter
32.	build up	aumentar	se fortifier
33.	burn down	quemarse	détruire par le feu
34.	burn up	quemarse	bruler entièrement
35.	burst out laughing	romper a reír	éclater de rire
36.	buy out	comprar la parte de	acheter un fonds
37.	by heart	de memoria	par Coeur
38.	by oneself	solo	tout seul

39.	call down	reganar	réprimander
40.	call off	cancelar	Annuler
41.	call up	llamar por teléfono	donner un coup de telephone
42.	catch cold	coger catarro	prendre froid
43.	catch fire	coger fuego	prendre feu
44.	catch on	entender, dares cuenta	y être
45.	carry out	llevar a cabo	exécuter
46.	check up	comprobar	verifier
47.	cheer up	alegrar, animar	rendre courage
48.	clean out	limpiar	néttoyer (à fond)
49.	come about	suceder	se produire
50.	come across	encontrarse con	rencontrer par hasard
51.	come to	volver en sí	se remettre
52.	count on	contrar con	compter sur

53.	cut off	cortar	couper
54.	die away	desparecer poco a poco	décroître peu à peu
55.	die down	acabarse, apagarse	se calmer
56.	die out	desaparecer, acabar	disparaître
57.	draw up	preparar	préparer
58.	drop out	dejar de asistir	quitter
59.	every so often	de vez en cuando	assez souvent
60.	fall in love with	enamorarse de	tomber amoureux de
61.	fall off	caerse, disminuir	tomber de
62.	feel like	tener ganas de	avoir envie de
63.	figure out	entender	imaginer
64.	fill out	llenar	remplir
65.	fool around	perder tiempo, bromear	perdre son temps
66.	for the time being	por ahora	pour le moment

being

67.	get along with	llevarse bien	s'entendre
68.	get even with	vengarse	se venger, rendre la pareille
69.	get in touch with	comunicarse con	comuniquer avec
70.	get on one's nerves	onerse nervioso	porter sur les nerfs
71.	get rid of	deshacerse de	se défaire de, se débarraser
72.	get the better of	aventajar	l'emporter sur
73.	get through	terminar, acabar	achever
74.	get used to	acostumbrarse	s'accoutumer
75.	give in	dares por vencido	se rendre à
76.	give someone a ring	llamar por telefono	donner un coup de téléphone à
77.	give up	dejar de, rendirse	se rendre
78.	go off	disparar, explotar	faire explosion

79.	go through	llevar a cabo, aprobarse	souffrir, subir
80.	go without saying	entenderse, sin decirse	il va sans dire que
81.	had better	es major que	il vaut mieux que
82.	hard of hearing	sordo	sourd d'oreille
83.	have it in for	tenerselas juradas a uno.	en vouloir à quelqu'un
84.	have on	tener puesto	porter
85.	have one's own way	salirse con la suya	en faire à sa tête
86.	have time off	tener tiempo libre	y être pour quelque chose
87.	hear of	oír hablar de	entendre parler de
88.	hold off	aguantar	se maintenir
89.	hold on	aguantar, detenerse	saisir, tenir
90.	hold up	robar	s'emparer de
91.	in a hurry	apurado	être pressé

92.	inside out-upside down	al revés	a l'envers
93.	in vain	en vano	en vain
94.	keep good time	andar bien	à l'heure
95.	keep house	hacer el trabajo del hogar	tenir maison, se mettre en ménage
96.	keep in touch with	mantenerse en contacto	continuer à
97.	keep in mind	recordar	se rappeler de
98.	keep out	no entre	ne pas entrer
99.	keep track of	llevar cuenta de	garder un record de
100.	keep up with	ir al paso de	aller aussi vite que
101.	lay off	dejar cesante, despedir	mettre au chomage
102.	let alone	dejar tranquilo para cuanto mas	laisser tranquille encore moins
103.	little by little	poco a poco	au fur et à mesure
104.	look after	cuidar	s'occuper de

105.	look out	tener cuidado	pendre garde
106.	look over	examinar	examiner, vérifier
107.	make believe	pretender	prétendre
108.	make fun of	burlarse de	se moquer de, se rire de
109.	make good time	viajar rápidamente	voyager vite, bien marcher (train)
110.	make out	salir bien, irle bien	réussir
111.	make over	reformar	refaire, remettre à la mode
112.	make up	compensar, inventar,	se réconcilier
113.	make up one's mind	decidir	prendre un parti
114.	never mind	no se preocupe	peu importe
115.	no matter	no importa	n'importe
116.	off and on	de vez en cuando	de temps à autre
117.	once and for all	una vez para siempre	une fois pour toutes

118.	once in a while	de vez en cuando	de temps en temps
119.	on time	a tiempo	à l'heure, à temps
120.	over and over	repetidamente	sans cesse
121.	play tricks on	tomarle el pelo	jouer un tour à quelqu'un
122.	put away	guardar	ranger
123.	put off	posponer	remettre
124.	put one' foot into	meter la pata	mettre les pieds dans le plat
125.	put out	apagar	éteindre, ériger
126.	quite a few	muchos	pas mal de
127.	right away	immediatamente	immédiatement
128.	run errands	hacer mandados	faire des courses
129.	sell-out	vender, liquidar	liquider
130.	set forth	salir, presantar	se mettre en chemin, exposer
131.	shake-hands	dar la mano	serrer la main, donner une

			poignée de mains
132.	show off	exhibirse, presumir	faire, parade de
133.	show up	presentarse	se présenter
134.	shut off	apagar	éteindre
135.	shut up	cerrar, callarse	se taire
136.	so far	hasta ahora	jusqu'à présent
137.	stand a chance	tener probabilidad	avoir la chance de
138.	stand out	sobresalir	se distinguer de
139.	stand to reason	es natural, claro	il va sans dire
140.	stand up for	salir en defensa de	prendre le parti de
141.	stick someone	engañar, estafar	tromper, voler
142.	stick up	sobresalir	se dresser
143.	take advantage of	aprovecharse de	profiter de
144.	take part	participar	participer à
145.	take a seat	tomar asiento	prendre un siége

146. take by surprise	sorprender	prendre au dépourvu
147. take for granted	dar por descontado	être persuadé
148. take into account	tener en cuenta	tenir compte de
149. take off	despegarse	partir
150. take one's time	tomar su tiempo	prendre son temps
151. take out	sacar	sortir
152. take over	tomar cargo de	se charger de
153. take pains	esmerarse	prendre de la peine
154. take pity on	tener lástima de	avoir pitié de
155. take place	tener lugar	avoir lieu
156. take something up with	consultar con	discuter avec
157. take time off	tomar tiempo	prendre un moment de loisir
158. take turns	alternarse	prendre chacun son tour

		son tour
159. talk over	discutir, tartar de	discuter
160. tear down	derribar	démolir
161. tear up	romper	déchirer
162. tell apart	distinguir entre	distinguer entre
163. tell time	saber el reloj	dire l'heure
164. think of	pensar de, parecerle	penser à
165. think over	pensarlo	réfléchir
166. think up	inventar, encontrar	inventer, imaginer
167. throw away	botar	jeter
168. throw up	vomitar	vomir
169. tired out	muy cansado	n'en plus pouvoir
170. to be over	terminado	être fini
171. to pick out	escoger	choisir
172. try on	probar	essayer

173. try out	probar	essayer
174. turn around	dar un vuelta	se retourner, faire volte face
175. turn down	rechazar	baisser
176. turn in	entregar, irse a la cama	aller se coucher; remettre
177. turn someone in	entregar a alguien	remettre
178. turn something in	entregare algo	rendre
179. turn someone on	excitar, gustar	allumer
180. turn someone off	repugnar, dar asco	éteindre
181. turn on someone	attacar, alguien	enthousiasmer
182. turn out	resultar	devenir
183. used to	soler	servir à, avoir l'habitude de
184. up to date	moderno al día	tenu à jour

185. wait on	servir	servir
186. wait up for	esperar, desvelandose	veiller
187. wait for	esperar	attendre
188. wake up	despertarse	s'éveiller, se réveiller
189. walk out (informal)	abandonar	abandonner
190. waste one's breath	perder el aliento	perdre son temps
191. wear down	gastar	user complètement
192. wear off	desaparecer	disparaitre (peu a peu)
193. wear out	gastarse	user
194. wear through	gastarse	user
195. work out	planear, resultar	bien finir, deviser
196. would rather	preferir	préférer
197. watch out for	tener cuidado con	faire attention à
198. walk out on someone or	abandonar	abandoner

something

199. write something off   anular   annuler

200. you bet   de acuerdo y como   d'accord

New English Grammar for ESL Students

Who is your better friend, Mickey or Janet?

Fritz-Meyer Sannon, PhD.

New English Grammar for ESL Students

Appendix E

U. S. States and Capitals

Alabama:	Montgomery	Montana:	Helena
Alaska:	Juneau	Nebraska:	Lincoln
Arizona:	Phoenix	Nevada:	Carson City
Arkansas:	Little Rock	New Hampshire:	Concord
California:	Sacramento	New Jersey:	Trenton
Colorado:	Denver	New Mexico:	Santa Fe
Connecticut:	Hartford	New York:	Albany
Delaware:	Dover	North Carolina:	Raleigh
Florida:	Tallahassee	North Dakota:	Bismarck
Georgia:	Atlanta	Ohio:	Columbus
Hawaii:	Honolulu	Oklahoma:	Oklahoma City
Idaho:	Boise	Oregon:	Salem
Illinois:	Springfield	Pennsylvania:	Harrisburg
Indiana:	Indianapolis	Rhode Island:	Providence
Iowa:	Des Moines	South Carolina:	Columbia

Fritz-Meyer Sannon, PhD.

Kansas:	Topeka	South Dakota:	Pierre
Kentucky:	Frankfort	Tennessee:	Nashville
Louisiana:	Baton Rouge	Texas:	Austin
Maine:	Augusta	Utah:	Salt Lake City
Maryland:	Annapolis	Vermont:	Montpelier
Massachusetts:	Boston	Virginia:	Richmond
Michigan:	Lansing	Washington:	Olympia
Minnesota:	St. Paul	West Virginia:	Charleston
Mississippi:	Jackson	Wisconsin:	Madison
Missouri:	Jefferson City	Wyoming:	Cheyenne

New English Grammar for ESL Students

About the Author

Fritz-Meyer Sannon has been teaching ESL for more than twenty-five years.

- Pace University

    Bachelors Degree (Academic)

- Queens College

    Masters Degree (Linguistics-literacy)

- New York University

    Scholarship and Fellowship (Doctoral Program /Linguistics)

- Fordham University

    Doctoral Program (language, literacy, learning)

    Book Scholarship

- International University for Graduate Studies

    PhD Degree (Language)

- Empire Institute

  Former Assistant Director

- Dyckman School of Languages

  Former Director Founder

- US Immigration Naturalization Service

  Former Interpreter-Translator (Creole, English, French, and Spanish)

- New York State Department of Social Services

  Former Management Specialist

- State University of New York/Queens EOC/York College

  Lecturer English Grammar

Publications:

- Réflexions d'un publiciste (France)
- Songs from Exile (U.S.A.)

Printed in the United States
29015LVS00002B/48